Christian Renewal in a Consumer Society

Written by Philip Evans

Foreword by Mark Prentice

'Christian Renewal in a Consumer Society'
written by Philip Evans.

ISBN: 0-9543907-9-2
ISBN-13: 978-0-9543907-9-2

This book is also available from Amazon for Kindle.

Published by the author.
13 Camborne Road, Welling, Kent,
United Kingdom DA16 3LD

Contact Philip Evans by e-mail at
philip.evans.gb@gmail.com

 Where Scripture quotations are in italics, the author has added the emphasis; where they include words in square brackets, these are clarifications added by the author.

Handling money and dealing with money problems can be complicated. Neither the author nor anyone else involved in the production or distribution of this book is responsible for any action you take, or fail to take, based on what is written in this book.

'It seems to me to be so much humbug to be praying [for revival] as we are praying, to be waiting as we are waiting, if we ourselves are not rightly related to God.'

Comment of a young man at a prayer meeting for church leaders during the early stages of the Hebrides Revival, 1950.

Humbug is frivolous or pretentious talk.

CONTENTS

'Philip's new book is timely and so very, very needed. When so many people are timid regarding the discussion of money, too many Christians find themselves in debt and are consequently in a severe bondage.

'I recommend this book because I know the author well and because it will help people. After you read it get copies to give away. Biblical to the core, his book is life-changing.

'If all Christians in Britain were to read this book it could even change the face of British Christianity.'

Dr R T Kendall

IF YOU HAVE MONEY PROBLEMS

If you have a money problem or debt, get help immediately. Although in an appendix I explain the basic skills needed to control money, finding out how to do it for the first time should not be left until you are in a crisis.

Changing the wheel on a car may seem very simple but stuck at the side of a busy road is not the best time to have to do it for the first time. Dealing with money problems and debt might seem simple enough but you should get expert help as soon as possible, to prevent things getting worse.

In many parts of the world, it is possible to get access to expert, independent advice from voluntary organisations. But remember that debt counsellors cannot do much to help you unless they know something about your overall financial situation, such as your income and major bills, because only then can they put together a practical repayment plan and negotiate with your creditors.

In the UK, we have some of the best independent, free, expert money advice available anywhere in the world. You will find local advice agencies listed in the front of telephone directories or at local libraries. Or you can call National Debtline on 0808 808 4000: calls are free from landlines and most mobile networks. Or look on these websites.

www.nationaldebtline.co.uk

www.citizensadvice.org.uk

adviceuk.org.uk

www.capuk.org

FOREWORD

It is a privilege to be asked to add the Foreword to Philip's latest contribution in the area of personal finance. Philip has an unusual knack of saying a great deal with great brevity and you would do well to read what follows slowly and prayerfully.

I first met Philip when we worked together in London. We were engaged in an exciting and challenging work and it became apparent that someone who had thought through the issues of personal finance and its place in Christian discipleship would be a valuable asset to the team. Philip was our man. It is hard to convey how much I appreciated his work. Quite apart from his impact on the ministry and outreach of the church, he challenged me at a personal level to think through my own relationship with money far more deeply than I had before – something for which I am profoundly grateful.

As you read this, you will quickly discover Philip's pastoral heart. He wants to bring you to Jesus, and to his teaching, and his power to redeem our relationship with our finances. This is a process as challenging as it is liberating. I learned from Philip that Jesus sees our relationship with money as one of the primary threats to our relationship with him – which is why he gave it so much attention. We simply cannot make progress in our own discipleship until we have negotiated and implemented our Lord's teaching, bringing our failures here, as elsewhere, to the cross in repentance and faith.

Along with some of his own teaching, Philip introduces us to others from previous generations who likewise grasped the significance of the issue before us. I commend this short book to you as you seek 'to be made new in the attitude of your minds, and to put on the new self, created to be like God in true righteousness and holiness'. It will guide you faithfully.

Rev'd Mark Prentice

Vicar of St John the Baptist with St Andrew, Ipswich
(Mission Ipswich East)

formerly Minister in Charge, All Souls Clubhouse
Community Centre & Church, London, 2004-2013

INTRODUCTION

Everyone knows there are a few hot-button topics that can make any conversation go nuclear. Religion. Health. Politics. Death. But when it comes to the most difficult conversation you can possibly have, a new survey from Wells Fargo & Co found one clear winner: money... Even the existentially terrifying topic of death, which you might expect to top such a survey, comes in second...

Chris Taylor, *The Last Taboo* (Reuters, 27 March 2014)

I began teaching personal finance in 2002. It was not something I had anticipated, and I was not at all certain that I wanted to make the career change, but it proved to be a wonderful job.

Personal financial education used to be called 'consumer education' and most of it is still designed to help people be active participants in our consumer society. It therefore leaves unchallenged many of society's assumptions and values.

The consumer society pressurises us to submit and fit in, to allow our individuality to be shaped by market forces. Almost everything has a price tag and the marketing is relentless and inescapable. But when we conform, we severely limit our ability to be true to ourselves. This is why it is important to talk about money and to think seriously about how we get and use it, no matter how uncomfortable it might make us feel.

Before I go any further, I must say that this book is an expanded edition of my book published early in 2018 as, *Money: What's to Know?* If you have read that book, you will find that everything there is reproduced here with few enhancements. But earlier this year, I realised there was something more to say and that is in Chapter 3, which is entirely new. The basic structure of the book is unchanged, with supplemental material in appendices, of which there are now two more. And this Introduction has been revised.

Even last year's *Money* book was itself a development of *Money: What's there to Teach*, that I produced in 2012, when I was based at All Souls Clubhouse Community Centre & Church in London – although the revision ended up twice the length and very different to that small black booklet.

But the original inspiration for all this writing was the book that helped me most when I began teaching personal finance: *The Seven Laws of Money*, by Michael Phillips. It was first published in 1974 but it is the author's abridged version published in 1993 that I read and which remains popular today. The important contribution of the book is that it is not just about the practical skills needed to handle money efficiently but how to live with money: 'how to get it, care for it and forget about it'. The seven laws follow the Taoist structure but it is not a religious book. (The author also wrote a book about business finance using ancient mythological-style deities he invented but it is not 'pagan' in its approach.) The *Seven Laws* helped me think through issues as I explored the Bible and, from that time, I wanted to write a book that mapped out a framework for living with money in a 'Christian' way. Although I have written other books, this one you are now reading finally fulfils that wish.

Many people have influenced my approach to financial education but perhaps none more so than Harper

Wright, who was head of financial education at MBNA Europe when I first met him and who continues to help people understand how to handle money well.

I am very grateful to the man who invited me to work at All Souls Clubhouse, Mark Prentice, for writing the Foreword. And to my friend and former pastor at Westminster Chapel, Dr R T Kendall, for his generous endorsement.

Without the help of three of my oldest friends, Emrys Lloyd-Roberts, Alan Connor and Martyn Barr, this book would have contained many more grammatical errors, tautologies and typos. I very much appreciate their support and encouragement.

If you have not already realised it, this book is based on the teachings of Jesus of Nazareth. He taught more about money and wealth than almost anything else. I am sure that his motive was so that his followers would not be deterred from living the way he described by the financial implications. If you are unfamiliar with Jesus' teaching and wondering what someone who lived 2,000 years ago could have said for our benefit today, please bear with me.

Jesus' biographers recorded that at the time people were 'astonished' at what he said because he spoke with authority, unlike their usual teachers. While he was still a teenager, his wisdom astounded the intellectuals at the Temple, the home and centre of Hebrew learning. When he returned there as an adult, they asked each other, 'How is it that this man has learning, when he has never studied?' They were, in effect, saying, *How come this country carpenter sounds like one of us?*

Throughout his time as a teacher, Jesus was challenged by theologians and politicians with trick questions, designed to get him into trouble with one or other of the ruling elites. But he always answered so adroitly that, each time, they had to give up. The first officers sent from the Temple to arrest him returned without him with the excuse, 'No one ever spoke like this man!' (Imagine police officers today sent to arrest a troublesome street preacher returning with that reason!) The Roman occupation authorities tried to remain above the controversy that surrounded Jesus but, in the end, the Governor was given little choice but to order Jesus to be executed as a dissident and heretic.

Jesus' authority did not come from wealth or family influence because he lacked both. His only education would have been in his home and at the local synagogue. But his words form a body of ancient wisdom as much worthy of our attention today as those left by Socrates, Confucius and Solomon. About a hundred years ago, an Anglican bishop said that he thought more people would be interested in Jesus as a person if they took the time to understand what he taught. I think that is true. Whether or not you are a Christian, I hope you will take the time to consider carefully what Jesus said about money.

I also refer to the letters of Paul of Tarsus. He was, unusually, by birth both a Jew and Roman citizen. As he was from Tarsus, he would have been familiar with Greek culture and philosophy. He trained as a Pharisee and was probably the one who did most to persecute the first Christians, until his own sudden conversion. He then gave up the chance of a glittering career in theology and politics to travel across the Roman Empire as an itinerant evangelist and apologist.

If the Bible is a new book to you, please keep in mind that it is not really a book but a library. It consists of history, theology, philosophy, poetry and correspondence written over a period of about 1,500 years. Moreover, it is a *religious* library, so that even the biographies should be read as *religious* history. It has had a wide-ranging impact on all sorts of people for thousands of years and I am convinced that it continues to help us today.

So that there is no misunderstanding, I should be clear that this book is not a guide to personal finance. While I include an explanation of why personal financial education is important, and an appendix explaining some basic money handling skills, this book is primarily an attempt to explain money and an appeal to develop a healthy relationship with it. I pray it will be a catalyst for spiritual renewal and revival.

Finally, if you are worried about your financial situation, or if you need help with debt, please see the information at the front of this book about getting free, independent, expert advice.

Philip Evans
New Year's Eve, 2019

1: SETTING THE SCENE

Ask the rich man, he'll confess,
Money can't buy happiness;
Ask the poor man, he don't doubt,
But he'd rather be miserable with than without.

Harold Rome, 'The Money Song' (1942)

Origins & Evolution

Money was invented in different parts of the world at different times but the first time may have been about 3,500 years ago, probably somewhere in China. The first types of money were everyday things like seashells and coloured beads. They did not need any intrinsic value of their own if everyone trusted and respected the system. This began to change only when the geographical areas within which people traded began to expand and their money needed to itself be something that everyone valued. When we read in Genesis that Jacob's sons took bundles of money from Canaan to Egypt to buy corn, it was probably silver rings of equal weight tied together in bundles of equal weight.

Banking and credit existed long before money and probably originated in ancient Babylon, where palaces and temples were the safest places to store precious metals, grain and fabrics. Even there, however, they were vulnerable, which is why Jesus of Nazareth referred to earthly treasures that moths and rust destroy or thieves break in and steal.

The earliest form of credit was probably the loan of seed to be repaid by a share of the harvest: these loans were made in the name of the ruler or deity associated with the 'bank'. This is what Joseph did in Egypt, towards the end of the seven years of famine, when he gave seed in Pharaoh's name in exchange for a fifth of the harvest.

The first coins were made at Lydia in Asia Minor in around the year 678 BC: the word 'money' derives from the name of the local goddess, Moneta. The Israelites first used coins about 100 years later, during or soon after their exile in Babylon. They may have been reluctant to use them because they would have been stamped with images of foreign rulers and pagan gods. Israel started to make its own coins in about 140 BC and the first moneychangers at the Temple may have provided a much appreciated service for visiting Jews by exchanging their foreign coins for ones they were happier to use.

An important change in the way people regarded money came about as it evolved from a convenient way to trade into a commodity that could itself be traded. In the ancient world, business investors usually received an agreed percentage of the actual profit made, not a fixed percentage of the amount of the loan. This was the same principle as before the creation of money, the same basis on which Joseph had loaned seed to farmers. It created a shared responsibility and risk, so that if a venture failed the lender lost the investment in the same way as the borrower lost all the work expended. This is why loans to relieve poverty were to be free of all profit: if lenders did charge interest, it was considered immoral and was probably illegal.

The Torah, God's 'Law' for the Israelites, forbade interest, except in the cases of foreign investment where shared responsibility and risk was not possible.[1] The only

---

[1] See Exodus 22:25, Leviticus 25:35-37 & Deuteronomy 23:19-20. I realise that these provisions are open to various other interpretations.

civilization in the ancient world known to allow interest routinely was Babylon.

The Roman Statesman, Cato, thought that convicted thieves should repay double the amount they stole but lenders who charged interest should repay four times as much! Most of the Church Fathers, the most influential theologians during the first 700 years of church history, thought charging interest despicable. Among them, Basil of Caesarea warned that those who charged interest added more to their sins than to their wealth and Augustine of Hippo thought their donations to the church dishonoured God.

Why was this? The old word for interest was usury and it means, literally, to sting like a serpent. That is how people used to think of interest! Today, most people understand usury to be *excessive* interest but, originally, it meant *all* interest. I first realised this when I began to research Islamic finance as part of my school presentations. Islamic finance observes the ancient prohibition on interest in the Koran, where it is called riba.[2]

Britain's King Henry VIII was the first European ruler to legalise interest but the move was repeatedly attacked until it was repealed. It was not until 30 years later that the Usury Act of 1571 enshrined in law the new meaning of usury – *excessive interest.* Gradually, charging interest began to lose its stigma and became one of the major building blocks of European civilisation.

Another significant stage in the evolution of money was to decrease its intrinsic value and to rely increasingly on the authority of the ruler who issued it. Henry VIII was, again, instrumental, because he seems to have been the

---

[2] A helpful modern explanation of the harm caused by interest is the 1999 Supreme Court of Pakistan's Judgment on Riba, written by Justice Muhammad Taqi Usmani.

first modern European ruler to replace the precious metal in coins with cheaper alternatives. (At least, he was the first to do it in an open, straightforward way, not trying to deceive people!)

In time, banknotes began to replace coins; later, plastic cards were all you needed.[3] Today, almost all money, probably over 98%, exists only as data in sophisticated computer systems that is transferred from one account to another without ever being issued as coins or notes.

It is not just governments and banks that create money. Cryptocurrencies can be produced within cyberspace by anyone with the necessary expertise and resources. As I write this, the most famous of these is Bitcoin, which is 'mined' in ways that parallel the mining of precious minerals, by decrypting data much as prospectors search the earth for gold and diamonds. This feat of human imagination and creativity has become every bit as valuable as anything people can dig out of the ground.

The creation of money was as important as the invention of the wheel. Without it, communities could not have expanded and the public services we take for granted today would have been impossible. But money has evolved beyond a tool, even an indispensable one. Economic theory is now regarded as a primary means of studying and explaining human life; the creation of wealth through capitalism is seen as the way to personal fulfilment. Money is the global status symbol that promises freedom, security, purpose, power and happiness. I have met many young people who thought that having a lot of money was necessary not only to

[3] Paper money (or, at least, money that looked like paper but was actually made out of various materials, including silk) was abandoned by the Chinese about 200 years before banknotes were introduced in Europe. The Chinese had never been able to effectively deter counterfeiting, even when each note warned of the mandatory death penalty.

marry and start a family but also to fall in love and be happy. Many people make the accumulation of money their life's goal; others use the things it can buy to define who they are. It is important to understand how this happened.

Towards Consumerism

Today, we understand capitalism as a political and economic system where goods and services are provided by private businesses trading for profit. It is virtually synonymous with democracy and often the only alternative is thought to be communism. But that was not how it began.

Throughout history, people have traded for profit but most of them did so only to make enough money to provide comfort and security for their families. Although there always were some traders who sought to maximise their business potential, making financial profit their supreme goal, even at the cost of ruining their rivals and exploiting their communities, it was not the usual business model. But from the middle of the 18th Century, what we now call capitalism gradually came to be seen as the preferred model for free trade. The change is often attributed to Benjamin Franklin (1706-1790), one of America's founding fathers. He made enough money to retire early and popularised his approach to business through articles that gradually found their way to almost every farmer and trader in America. He taught that money, not labour, created wealth. And while he stopped short of equating leisure with idleness, that was the impression he created.

> *Remember, that Time is Money. He that can earn Ten Shillings a day by his labour, and goes abroad, or sits idle, one half of that day, though he spends but Sixpence during his Diversion or Idleness, ought not to reckon That the only expense; he has*

> *really spent, or rather thrown away, Five Shillings besides...*
>
> *Remember, that Money is of the prolific, generating Nature. Money can beget Money, and its Offspring can beget more, and so on. Five Shillings turned, is Six: Turned again, 'tis Seven and Three Pence; and so on 'til it becomes an Hundred Pound. The more there is of it, the more it produces every Turning, so that the Profits rise quicker and quicker. He that kills a breeding Sow, destroys all her Offspring to the thousandth Generation. He that murders a Crown [a coin worth Five Shillings], destroys all that it might have produced, even Scores of Pounds.*

Franklin's view that money is fertile – that money should begat money – would have appalled Christians a thousand years earlier. In fact, it is surprising that even in 18th Century America it was not more widely condemned as the sin of avarice, the love of money! But Franklin's logic and humour shaped not only business practice but a way of life. That is why the USA puts his picture on its $100 bills. But although he did no more than advocate an intensely logical approach to business, it inspired greed; in time, his way became the only way to do business.

Capitalism thrives on consumerism. This is an economy that grows by encouraging people to borrow to buy an ever increasing variety of goods and services. In 1899, Thorstein Veblen wrote, *The Theory of the Leisure Class*, which sought to justify the purpose in life of rich people as being no more than consuming what others produce. The title of Dr Veblen's most famous book, *Conspicuous Consumption*, has become part of the English language: the open accumulation of luxury goods and services in order to enhance social status.

During the Industrial Revolution, the development of a 'middle class' bridged the huge gap that had previously separated workers and nobility. The allure of consumerism soon began to inspire this new class of people keen to improve their social standing. During the 1980s, new IT innovations made possible a credit explosion, so that even people in varying degrees of poverty could begin to buy what they could not afford.

Consumer credit today is something that I doubt many people living 150 years ago ever dreamed about. The idea of routinely, habitually borrowing money simply to gratify passing desires would, I am sure, have seemed beyond reckless. As there was nothing like consumer credit in ancient Israel, I have heard some say that the ancient prohibition on interest on loans has no relevance today. While I see the logic of that, consumer credit makes greed and covetousness possible and that dangerous freedom underpins many of our assumptions and attitudes about life and today's entitlement culture.

The Way We Live Now

Although many people today want to see the pursuit of business profit moderated by other considerations, in many parts of the world the responsibility to maximise profit is a legal requirement. And while many businesspeople trade honestly, the diversity of goods and services they trade far exceeds what people need to live healthy, comfortable lives and serves only to exploit greed and addiction. This too often incurs the expense of needless credit and increases the risk of uncontrollable debt. It takes more than a few paragraphs to sum up the situation today but the following sets the scene.

- Money is so important in almost every area of life that it is very difficult to express the value of anything except as price or cost.
- The price of goods and services is not determined by the cost of production but by the demand that can be created for them. As a result, basic foods

like milk are often sold below the cost of production, so that farmers have to be subsidised to stay in business, while luxury goods and 'must haves' can be sold at huge profit.

- Goods and services are available 24/7: assuming you can pay the price, you can have what you want at any time of the year, from anywhere in the world.
- Psychology has empowered marketing, advertising and sales talk to exploit basic human needs like security, self-esteem and significance. This is used to manipulate us into buying what we neither need nor previously wanted.
- Information Technology has made 'instant' credit possible, so that we can act on a whim to buy what we cannot afford.
- People like city brokers and bankers, whose skill is trading money to make money, are more highly valued and highly paid than people in healthcare, education and social services.
- Shopping is a leisure activity: it is often the first diversion that comes to mind when we are bored and a favourite way to spend time with friends.
- As acquisition has become so important to personal self-esteem and social worth, 'honesty' has become increasingly subjective.

It may be useful if I elaborate on the final point. Some forms of deceit are so commonplace, we no longer think of them as dishonest but simply the way we do things today. Salespeople cold-call us, claiming to be conducting or following up surveys; others claim they know about our credit deals, phone contracts and computer problems. Harassment is routine, especially when call centres are located in countries where they are not regulated and automated dialling systems ring the same numbers three, four or more times in a day, from early morning to late evening.

Representatives from utility companies visit our homes claiming to be investigating the misuse of tariffs but really want us to switch to them. Building companies send people to conduct property inspections but they are really touting for work. These salespeople can introduce themselves using carefully chosen words designed to create the impression they have some official status or are acting on behalf of a government agency.

This approach has infiltrated domestic life and led to high levels of personal dishonesty. Putting false information on credit applications and inventing or inflating insurance claims is widespread. High majorities of people admit to pilfering from employers, restaurants and hotels. I was surprised recently to hear how much linen and medical equipment is stolen from State funded (NHS) hospitals in the UK!

Our 'default position' when looking for tradesmen and other service providers is to expect to be cheated with poor service or over-charging; when we complain about faulty goods or deficient work, we expect to be treated with suspicion, as if we are making it up.

Sadly, the situation seems to be no different among Christians. I have met some in business who believe that if something is not illegal it cannot be sinful. It is still worse when they are engaged in charitable or church work. It seems as if their subjective certainty in the rightness of their divine 'calling' trumps any objective code of conduct derived from the Scriptures and they see nothing inappropriate or improper in resorting to deception, deceit and dishonesty.

At a personal level, occasionally I have been asked to help Christians with money problems, only to discover they were fiddling their tax return or Benefit claim or had got credit deceitfully. Christians who would not *lie* on their CVs nonetheless boast of their abilities and achievements with little objectivity and no concern for the Christian virtues of modesty and humility. And to look at many of their fashion statements and social media posts, you might wonder what difference their allegiance to Jesus Christ makes to their lifestyles and ambitions.[4]

Many church ministers do not dare to talk about money for fear of creating a wrong impression about themselves or their churches. This is true, even when their churches struggle to pay the bills! Others restrict their teaching on giving only to those times of the year when they hope to encourage their congregations to exceed their regular giving, such as on annual 'gift' days. As disappointing as this is, there is some good teaching by ministers who deliver it with no ulterior motive. But, even then, good teaching is not enough.

Change comes only when people act on what they hear but, when it comes to money, this usually requires doing the uncomfortable, if not unthinkable: it means giving up old ways of earning, saving and spending money. Yet a failure to act is serious enough to leave us deluded about both our humanity and our faith.

Money: Tool or Tyrant?

People have always failed to control money adequately. In *A History of Money*, Professor Glyn Davies observed that, 'Despite man's growing mastery of science and technology, he has so far been unable to master money, at any rate with any acceptable degree of success, and to the extent that it has succeeded, the irrecoverable costs in terms of mass unemployment and lost output would seem

[4] Consider, for example, Proverbs 27:2, Romans 12:3, Philippians 2:3, James 4:6 & 1 Peter 5:5.

to outweigh the benefits.' Why is this? The problem has engaged better minds than mine but here is my opinion.

Although money has objective power, it is not real. As I explained previously, almost all of it exists only as computer data. It is therefore a system of trust and its presence in the world has the same sort of reality as a novel: it is 'real' only in that it gives expression to the idea. This is why it is impossible to control. The best we can do is to try to influence the factors that control money.

Individuals can have significant control over their income and spending, yet we all make mistakes and behave a little foolishly from time to time. Also, we are all subject to events beyond our control, such as illness and redundancy or when things break down and have to be repaired or replaced. Or the sudden depreciation of our savings, investments and pension plans. And, ultimately, no amount of money can protect us from death!

It is more complex for families to control money, because of the diverse needs and behaviour of the individual members; it is still harder for companies and nations. The Eurozone seems to go from one crisis to another because the range of conflicting factors is beyond the influence of any one government or institution.

Although we try to make fiction real in many ways, it is never really real and the extent to which it affects our lives depends on how we relate to it. We make novels seem more real by turning them into television programmes and films, so we can watch people act out the stories. We produce reference books that describe the fiction as if it were real, like biographies of Sherlock Holmes and tour guides for Tolkien's Middle-Earth. We can get more involved when the fiction becomes a computer game, where we are part of the story and our own abilities and preferences affect the plot. People can even create wholly fictional lives for themselves by means of avatars living in virtual worlds imagined in cyberspace.

When people are obsessed with fiction, they can become unbalanced in real life: they cease to make clear distinctions about what is important or understand what acceptable behaviour is. In the same way, obsession with money often changes people for the worse, distorting their perceptions and priorities. Also, medical research has shown that making money can produce the same sort of 'high' as cocaine, by stimulating the same area of the brain. All this goes some way to explaining the escalating selfishness, greed and recklessness that drives people to sacrifice their relationships, neglect their families and ruin their health for money!

This danger of intoxication is why 'wealth gurus' often advise people to define the lifestyle they want and then work out how rich they need to be to live it, rather than to risk ruining their lives driven by an abstract concept of what it means to be rich. But Jesus of Nazareth had something even more malevolent in mind when he said that we cannot serve both God and money.

Money & Mammon

Actually, Jesus did not say that we cannot serve both God and money. He said, 'God and *mammon*'. Although some Bibles translate the word mammon as 'money', there is a difference. Money is a tool for living but mammon is the power in money that influences people. This might sound as if money can acquire personality and achieve a will of its own and, in the past, some Christians have thought of mammon as a demon. But it is an impersonal force, like the force of an idea whose time has come. The ways people relate to money gives it power over them. And when enough people think that way, everyone else has little choice but to do the same.

Jesus said that we cannot serve both God and mammon at least twice: once in his Sermon on the Mount, his description of a lifestyle that is in step with the world that God made, and again when he was confronted by some religious leaders who claimed to serve God but really loved money.[5] Crucially, he was not saying that it is immoral or dangerous to try serving both God and mammon; rather, he was explaining that it is impossible. 'For either he will hate the one and love the other', Jesus explained on both occasions, 'or he will be devoted to the one and despise the other.'

The truth is that both God and mammon have the ability to captivate our devotion. In fact, we cannot even hope to serve our own best interests if we submit to the power of money, which is why I hope you will continue reading even if you are not a Christian.

Mammon is a concept that originated in ancient Babylon. Historians used to look back to Rome or Greece for the seeds of modern civilisation but increasingly they now look further back, to Babylon. The city is now an archaeological and cultural site in modern Iraq, on the River Euphrates, about 60 miles south of Baghdad, but in ancient history it dominated two great empires. Since then, it has been an enduring symbol of great wealth, culture, learning, self-indulgence and decadence.

In America during 'the roaring 20s', a time of unprecedented economic growth and prosperity, George S Casson began writing the first modern self-help leaflets explaining how to get rich, using stories about people living in ancient Babylon. His characters included Bansir, a chariot maker who desired gold, a wise old merchant called Kalabab and Arkad, said to be the richest man in Babylon. These leaflets were distributed in such large quantities by banks and insurance companies, they

---

[5] See Matthew 6:24 & Luke 16:13.

became familiar to millions of people. The advice in them includes seven cures for a lean purse and the five laws of gold.

In 1926, the stories were collated in a book called, *The Richest Man in Babylon*, and it remains an inspirational classic. In the Foreword, Casson wrote, 'Babylon became the wealthiest city of the ancient world because its citizens were the richest people of their time. They appreciated the value of money. They practiced sound financial principles in acquiring money, keeping money and making their money earn more money. They provided for themselves what we all desire ... incomes for the future.' Casson was a publisher, not a historian, but he drew on archaeological evidence to reinforce the popular belief that ancient Babylon, the oldest known civilisation, was a capitalist society!

One interesting point of similarity between ancient Babylon and now is how in Babylon business profits and losses were recorded on clay tablets. The profit from one business venture, such as a trading expedition, could therefore be reinvested into another without ever being turned into physical wealth.

Although there were no idols called mammon in Babylon, and no temples dedicated to it, life there revolved around money as if it were the State religion. This way of thinking has continued down through the centuries. Many historians believe that major world events, such as wars, voyages of discovery and technological advances were the product of financial pressures and innovations; others go further and believe that they were the consequence of simple greed manipulating people's self-interest.

Consider this paradox. We live in a world that has never been so free to create wealth. Although money is essentially a system of trust and no longer founded on the need to accumulate gold or other physical wealth, we have never been so limited in our ability to create more. Quantitative easing is what Governments and central banks call creating new money arbitrarily in order to avoid problems: it is the modern equivalent of printing money. Digital mining is the way to discover cryptocurrencies: the modern equivalent of digging for gold. They must be micromanaged, however, to avoid triggering much greater problems, like rampant inflation and economic collapse.

But inflation is not an automatic or inevitable consequence of creating new money. It is the product of greed. If the people worked collectively for the common good, the new money would work for them all, albeit indirectly. You may say, *That will never happen!* I agree. But I am not expressing a hope but making a point. It is the love of money that is the problem, not the money itself.

Jesus never put anything in opposition to God in the same way as he put the power of money. He did not say, for example, that we cannot serve both God and sex, even though throughout the Bible the two things that repeatedly compromised people's faith in God were sexual misconduct and material greed.[6] Does this imply that Jesus gave a higher priority to handling money than to sexual behaviour? Arguably. Personally, I think he did give it a higher priority: not because financial sin is greater or the consequences more severe but because the

---

[6] The Bible refers to both sexual and financial misconduct as fornication or prostitution and most times it is financial. The word often translated 'unfaithfulness' towards the end of Psalm 73 is the Hebrew word meaning prostitution but it has nothing to do with sex because the entire Psalm is about people who prosper in spite of their wickedness. James in his letter to the churches calls his readers 'adulterers and adulteresses' but he was writing about their love of money.

risks are more subtle and people are more easily deceived into thinking they are doing nothing wrong.

Money does not take control of society; society gives it control. Mammon is the power that society has given to money and it operates in the background of life, often many steps removed from the action, like a pagan idol.

The Root of Infidelity

When Jesus warned against trying to serve both God and mammon, he knew the truth that Paul of Tarsus later articulated so memorably: the love of money is the root of all evil.[7]

> *Those who desire to be rich fall into temptation, into a snare, into many senseless and harmful desires that plunge people into ruin and destruction. For the love of money is a root of all kinds of evils. It is through this craving that some have wandered away from the faith and pierced themselves with many pangs.*

As you can see in this quotation, the English Standard Version of the Bible (ESV) that I quote in this book, like many modern translations, says that the love of money is '*a* root of *all kinds* of evils'. This is, I think, a consequence of so many generations of Christians growing up in a society that takes for granted capitalism and consumerism. We have come to see Paul's words as a general observation that, like all generalisations, is not entirely accurate. Although I find the ESV a particularly helpful translation, in view of everything else in the Bible about money and wealth, I think the traditional rendering of 1 Timothy 6:8 more accurately conveys Paul's warning: *the* love of money is *the* root of *all* evil!

It is not necessary to take literally the Bible's explanation of the origin of evil to see this. In Isaiah 14,

---

[7] 1 Timothy 6:9-10.

we read words originally attributed to Nebuchadnezzar, King of Babylon, but which many theologians think are applicable to Lucifer, the angel that rebelled against God and became the devil.

> *You said in your heart, 'I will ascend to heaven; above the stars of God I will set my throne on high; I will sit on the mount of assembly in the far reaches of the north; I will ascend above the heights of the clouds; I will make myself like the Most High'.*

In Genesis 3, we read about the origin of evil in the world when the devil, in the guise of a serpent, enticed the first woman, Eve, into eating the fruit that God had forbidden to her and her husband.

> *But the serpent said to the woman, 'You will not surely die. For God knows that when you eat of it your eyes will be opened, and you will be like God, knowing good and evil'.*

Crucially, neither Lucifer nor Eve wanted to be God: what they both wanted was to be *like* God. Pride is often said to be the beginning of all sin. Thomas Aquinas (1225-1274) wrote, 'It is characteristic of pride to be unwilling to be subject to any superior, and especially to God...' You might be thinking, *But what did money have to do with that?* Since humans invented it, money has made egotism possible. With money, we can seek to gratify the same feelings of pride and greed that Lucifer and Eve felt.

In many ways, Lucifer had it all. But he had it in dependence on God and he was jealous of God's autonomy. Eve and her husband lived idyllically in the Garden of Eden but they focussed more on what they could not have, the one fruit forbidden to them.

Egotism motivated Nebuchadnezzar as it had Lucifer. He did more than any other king of Babylon to beautify the city and to enhance its reputation for wealth and culture. And he desired to conquer God's special city, the holy city of Jerusalem.

It was the same sense of self-sufficiency and self-fulfilment that the devil sought to provoke when he tempted Jesus in the wilderness. In James' letter, he referred to the boasting of the business people who made their plans for prosperity without reference to God not as misguided or arrogant but as 'evil'![8]

Money is what people use to meet their needs and fulfil their ambitions; it is their way of getting things and getting things done; it is how they make their way in society and their mark on history. It is what they turn to when they turn away from God; it is what they must rely on when they will not rely on God. Physical strength, social superiority, media influence, military might and political skill can be used to control people but money buys it all.

Today the love of money lures people into indifference, disloyalty, deceit and fraud. At extremes, they do not care who gets hurt when they lie to discredit colleagues to get promotions, liquidate viable businesses for short-term profit or deal in legal highs,[9] drugs and child pornography.

Real Dangers

As money has such power, our attitude to it is as crucial to our emotional and spiritual well-being as our skill in handling it. This is why people of all religions struggle with these issues.[10] Psychologists have found that people

---

[8] See Matthew 4:1-11, Luke 4:1-13 & James 4:13-16.

[9] These are concoctions of psychoactive substances that are not illegal but produce similar effects to cocaine, cannabis, ecstasy and other illegal drugs.

[10] In thinking through my own position as a Christian, I have found very helpful books written by authors from various

with 'loose' attitudes towards money tend to be happier than those who are more controlling. Nevertheless, they are no less likely to be materialists, and no less prone to overspending and debt, and therefore just as vulnerable to the same problems.

Research has shown that people with money problems are less competent because the mental and emotional burden blunts their creativity, intuitiveness and productivity. Research has found that university students with money problems, struggling to make ends meet, do less well in their final exams than expected.

This is all on top of the more fundamental and widespread problems caused by materialism. Dr Oliver James, a psychologist and the author of *Affluenza* and *The Selfish Capitalist*, explains how people with an undue emphasis on money, possessions, entertainments, appearances and status are particularly vulnerable to emotional disorders. This can plunge them into a downward spiral, as they seek to relieve their feelings of insecurity, inadequacy and depression by buying what they think will bring relief and happiness.

When I taught in schools, I often began by asking the pupils what careers they were considering. Sometimes, someone would explain their choice by saying that it is a way to make a lot of money; just occasionally, one would say that they would do *any* job that made them rich. I usually explained that while there is nothing wrong in doing a job you love that pays well, and that may make you rich, if your primary goal is to be rich, it is almost certain that you will be a very different person by the time you achieve it. You will be changed by the skills you will need to acquire and by the suspicions, rivalries and betrayals you will endure. Of course, you will experience

---

religious traditions, including Buddhists, Muslims and Jews, together with authors with no discernible religious convictions.

these things whatever you decide to do in life, but you will find it very much worse because of money's power over people.

When you begin to accumulate money, you will suddenly become much more credible to many people. Just because you have money. Your opinions will be listened to and your jokes will be laughed at. And you will be envied. The strategies you will evolve for relating to people will almost certainly corrode your personality. As your views narrow and your attitudes harden, people will not tell you. They may not even notice. Just because you have money. And as your behaviour erodes, they may just turn a blind eye. Because you have money.[11] And you may well end up unable to enjoy your wealth because, by then, you will have become isolated and insulated, conditioned to the race and unable to feel satisfied with anything. This does not happen to everyone but it seems to happen to most.

By describing the love of money as a root, Paul illustrated how it ruins lives. A root is an ugly tangle that grows underground, out of sight, from where it anchors and feeds flowers and fruit that look and taste very different. It follows that if you want to look for avarice in your life, do not dig around for the root in the darkness of your unconscious mind but look for the fruit and flowers in your behaviour: greed or gluttony, for example, or possessiveness, jealousy, vanity, snobbery, arrogance, extravagance, ostentation, pretension, judgementalism, indifference or selfishness.

[11] This is how celebrity abuse against women and children was able to continue for decades. As terrible as that abuse is, I believe we should be just as worried by the complacency of the people who chose to ignore it, especially when they kept silent because of the financial consequences to themselves and their organisations of speaking out.

Voices from the Past

Church history is full of warnings about the love of money, called avarice, and the desire for things, called covetousness. They were considered to be 'deadly' sins. They were deadly because they could kill your soul, the real you, kill your relationships with others and kill your relationship with God. The demons of avarice and covetousness were portrayed in the front line of the devil's army because they wounded believers, leaving them vulnerable to pride, jealousy, greed, gluttony, anger, selfishness, deceit, indifference and even cruelty. In the 4th Century, John Chrysostom wrote this.

> *For a dreadful, a dreadful thing is the love of money, it disables both eyes and ears, and makes men worse to deal with than a wild beast, allowing a man to consider neither conscience, nor friendship, nor fellowship, nor the salvation of his own soul, but having withdrawn them at once from all these things, like some harsh mistress, it makes those captured by it its slaves. And the dreadful part of so bitter a slavery is, that it persuades them even to be grateful for it...*

In 1886, the Baptist preacher C H Spurgeon made a similar point about covetousness.

> *Covetousness breeds insensibility in the heart, a mortification in the conscience, a blindness in the mind! It is as hard to convict a man of it as to make a deaf ear hear of its own deficiencies. You cannot make a horseleech see the impropriety of desiring to suck – to all your expostulations it renders the one answer, 'Give, give'.*

While the challenge for all of us who grew up in the consumer society is to see the extent to which we are deaf to our deficiencies and slaves to the social norms, I think it is even more acute for people in business. In his book,

Discipleship, published in 1897, G Campbell Morgan devoted a chapter to work. This extract about business behaviour is no less relevant today.

> *No disciple of Jesus can amass a fortune simply for the sake of possession. He may be prosperous in his undertakings, but his prosperity must ever mean increased opportunity for Divine service. No disciple can oppress the hireling in his wages. That wage should be, not merely the measure of keeping his servant's body and soul together, it should include provision for the culture of all that his being demands. A 'living wage' in the common acceptation of that term, is not the measure for a Christian paymaster.*
>
> *A Christian cannot consent to enrich himself by taking advantage of the downfall or misfortune of another man. That man who strikes a bargain to his own profit which takes advantage of some pressing need on the part of another, is none of Christ's... The twofold law of life, enunciated by our Teacher, will purify commerce throughout, and nothing short of that will ever do it. 'Thou shalt love the Lord thy God with all thy heart, and with all thy soul, and with all thy mind...Thou shalt love thy neighbour as thyself.'*

Dr Morgan then continued with inspirational words about Jesus' teaching that apply to all of life, not just business.

> *These are said to be impossible ideals for business life today.* ***We reply that the very essence and genius of discipleship is the realisation of the impossible.*** *It is just because the Church of Jesus Christ has stood in the presence of his teaching and said 'Impossible' that she has become so weak and forceless in all the affairs of this busy age. Let us have a few men and women again who, like the*

early disciples in Pentecostal days, believe in Jesus and in the eternal wisdom of all His teaching, and who are prepared to suffer the loss of all things rather than disobey, and the potency and possibility of His ideals will begin to dawn on the world again as it did in those days, breaking up dynasties, revolutionising empires, and turning the world upside down.

Asherah: An Allegory

In the Old Testament, we read how the Canaanites put carved poles in their fields to honour their fertility goddess,[12] Asherah, in the hope of getting a good harvest and increasing their flocks. God told the Israelites to tear down and burn these poles when they moved in. And in what seems a strange prohibition, God forbade erecting Asherah poles near altars dedicated to himself. Yet, whether the Israelites simply followed what their pagan neighbours did in the belief that it was sound agricultural practice, or whether they were hedging their bets by honouring the local deity, the Israelites did just what God had forbidden. I expect that, were we able to ask some of them, they would say that they had not turned away from the true God and would deny trying to serve both God and Asherah.

Asherah divided the Israelites' loyalties, just as money divides the loyalties of Christians today. Preachers often say that God is more important than money, something impossible for any Christian to disagree with, but the problem is not that money might be more important but that we think it sufficiently important to divert our attention and compromise our allegiance to God.

Another parallel make be helpful. In Corinth, some Christians attended pagan festivals. In his letter to the

[12] Living trees were also carved for the same reason.

church there, Paul asked, 'Shall we provoke the Lord to jealousy?' We might wonder why those Christians would have ever wanted to attend pagan shrines, participate in pagan festivals and knowingly eat food that had been sacrificed to idols. Well – actually, I expect there were many reasons that are very familiar to us today. I am speculating, of course, but I think they went because they were the civil occasions and business networks of their day. And those Christians had a rationale to justify their behaviour: they dismissed the pagan practices as just superstition. After all, they reasoned, 'an idol has no real existence'. In other words, that they were not gods able to bless or curse. Paul agreed with that assessment but gave two good reasons why the Corinthians should stay away.

First, they were causing real problems for the Christians whose faith was not 'strong' enough to understand such behaviour. I imagine those 'weaker' Christians must have had a hard time if they had worshipped at those shrines in the past, before they believed on the Lord Jesus Christ. Perhaps some of them, both men and women, may have been shrine prostitutes and wondered how any Christian could bear to be associated with such activities! Second, Paul explained how the devil utilises people's devotion to idols and wanted the Christians to steer clear of anything demonic: 'what pagans sacrifice they offer to demons and not to God. I do not want you to be participants with demons'.

Paul exposed the belief that Christians who wanted to get on in society and succeed in business need to compromise with the norms of behaviour in their social and work environments. But like the Israelite farmers who put Asherah poles in their fields, the Christians at Corinth signalled that they did not believe – not really believe – that God could or would achieve as much for them! Today, some rationalise their compromise by thinking that if they are respected in society and business they will be both 'salt' and 'light', to use Jesus' metaphors for how Christians can impact society. But by their compromise, they lose the ability to be either or make much of a difference at all.

There is no middle ground between the lifestyle that Christ Jesus described for his disciples and the generally accepted norms of capitalism and the consumer society. Although generations of Christians have believed that capitalism is 'divinely ordained', any system that gives primacy to money is contrary to God's ways. This is why the influence of money today is as dangerous to Christian witness as any Canaanite goddess or Corinthian idol.

Meeting the Challenges

I wrote in the Introduction that most personal financial education is designed to help people participate fully in the consumer society without tipping into uncontrollable debt. Even with no higher goal, it can achieve a great deal of good, equipping and empowering people to make their own good choices and to understand the limits of their own competence.

Although a salesperson may explain savings plans, credit deals, insurance policies or mobile phone tariffs fairly, potential customers need to be able to evaluate that information. And just as when trying to fix a computer problem or a car engine, it is good to know when to give up trying to sort out money problems and seek expert help. Many debt repayment plans negotiated by debt advisers fail within about six weeks because the people in debt did not properly understand their predicament or give their advisers enough good information about their overall situation.

Effective financial education motivates changes in behaviour, such as creating a budget, reducing credit card and overdraft balances, saving, planning for retirement and starting an emergency fund that reduces dependence on credit and insurance. It should result in people having fewer liabilities and increased net worth. Research has suggested that people who act on financial education are, after about ten years, on average better off by a whole year's income.

My own approach began to take shape when I read Professor Davies' book and his observation that 'just when physical scientists are seeing the value of a more humanistic approach, economics, and particularly monetary economics, has become less so by attempting to become more "scientific", mechanistic and measurable'. Although he was considering the big picture, I saw that a fully human approach was necessary for personal finance. As I used to explain to school teachers, there is little point in telling young people how to use credit cards properly if we do not also show them how to evaluate the pressures on them to spend and to develop the skills and self-discipline necessary to spend wisely.

I therefore began with the need for people to understand themselves well enough to handle their money in their own best interests. We daily face an army of advertisers and salespeople trying to sidestep our rationale and target our emotions. This is often achieved by provoking discontent with who we are and what we have, so we will buy new clothes, cosmetics, fashion accessories, gadgets, entertainments and holidays in the hope of feeling better about ourselves. But we can spend money only once, so when we have been persuaded to spend it in ways that suit other people, we cannot use it to meet our own priorities or develop our unique character and abilities.

At the heart of what I taught was this paradox. While nobody should buy a chocolate bar, a bike or anything else without the money to pay for it, nobody should give up on a dream simply because they do not have the money to make it happen. This is not blind optimism but simply how the world works. We rely too much on money and, very often, much can be done without it. And, when money is needed, people may respond positively and supportively to our commitment. But this falls far short of what Jesus calls us to.

To what extent does your Christian commitment guide the ways you handle money?

- Do you contribute to the maintenance of your local church? People of all religions contribute to their local meeting place. And many others subscribe to social clubs, sports clubs and gyms.
- Do you support Christian outreach, the relief of poverty and other charitable works? The followers of many religions contribute towards its spread and many others contribute financially to political parties and social causes.
- Are you diligent at work, not exaggerating your expenses claims or claiming unwarranted overtime, not pilfering office stationery or other resources? I doubt you are unique.
- Do you refrain from excessive credit commitments and always plan to pay what you owe on time and in full? Many people, rich and poor, learn the necessary personal financial skills to manage their money sensibly.
- Are you content with fewer lifestyle accessories than your neighbours? Are you less concerned than your friends to keep up with fashions and trends? Such contentment is not a uniquely Christian trait.

Jesus' teaching about money goes further than this and what lies at its heart is not a paradox but a conundrum. When he said that we cannot serve both God and mammon, the power of money, because to do so is impossible, that seems simple enough. But he also said that we are to use mammon in ways that show that we do not serve mammon: to use the power without being influenced by it. And that is easier said than done!

Jesus did not despise money or suggest that we could be careless with it. Paul knew the value of money to fund ministry and relieve hardship. But neither Jesus nor any of his apostles depended on money and there is no suggestion that any of them might have achieved more if they had been wealthier!

The value of Jesus' teaching is not simply his wisdom but his ability to see life from a distance. It is something like the 'overview effect' that significantly changes the perspective of astronauts, who have looked down on our world in its entirety and wondered how we can pollute it and fight each other for a small piece of it. Jesus' perspective allows us to see something of the big picture and put into context the things that seem to us so immediate and important. Please read on to discover what he said.

2: A BETTER PARADIGM

You shall love the Lord your God with all your heart, and with all your soul, and with all your mind, and with all your strength. This is the first commandment. The second is this, You shall love your neighbour as yourself. There is no other commandment greater than these.

Jesus of Nazareth

Foundation & Paradigm

To understand what Jesus taught about money, we must first understand something of what he taught about life. We cannot separate the ways we get and use money from the ways we think about what it is to be human and how we should live together in community.

Matthew and Mark[13] both describe the time a religious lawyer asked Jesus to identify the greatest commandment in the Torah, Israel's 'Law'. Matthew says this was intended to test Jesus but, reading both accounts, it seems to have been a benevolent test. By that, I mean the lawyer came upon the group arguing with Jesus but asked a genuine question. I think the lawyer wanted to understand where Jesus was coming from, to better understand everything else he taught. The answer Jesus gave is at the start of this chapter.

---

[13] See Matthew 22:35-40 & Mark 12:28-34.

In an incident that Luke records,[14] another religious lawyer asked Jesus, 'Teacher, what shall I do to inherit eternal life?' This time, Jesus asked the lawyer to state his own opinion. The lawyer replied with a summary very similar to what Jesus had said previously: 'You shall love the Lord your God with all your heart and with all your soul and with all your strength and with all your mind, and your neighbour as yourself'. Jesus told him, 'You have answered correctly; do this, and you will live'.

It is no surprise that the second lawyer gave the same answer that Jesus had given earlier. Academics and lawyers often discussed what principles lay at the heart of the Torah and Jesus' summary may not have been unique to him. Even if it had been, the lawyer may have heard Jesus' followers and critics discussing it.

The Sermon on the Mount does not include the command to love God and love our neighbours but that is the lifestyle it describes. In the following extract, we have Jesus' paradigm for handling money.[15]

> *No one can serve two masters, for either he will hate the one and love the other, or he will be devoted to the one and despise the other. You cannot serve God and money. Therefore I tell you, do not be anxious about your life, what you will eat or what you will drink, nor about your body, what you will put on. Is not life more than food, and the body more than clothing? Look at the birds of the air: they neither sow nor reap nor gather into barns, and yet your heavenly Father feeds them. Are you not of more value than they? ... But seek first the kingdom of God and his righteousness, and all these things will be added to you.*

A paradigm is a framework that helps us to understand

[14] See Luke 10:25-28.

[15] Matthew 6:24-33.

something. Jesus' paradigm for money has three principles.

- Do not worry or fret about material things like food and clothing – or anything else that money can buy.[16]
- Make seeking God's Kingdom and righteousness the sole lifestyle priority, living as Jesus described elsewhere in the Sermon.
- Trust God for basic needs.

Paul of Tarsus was ideally suited by his background and training to relate Jesus' teaching to people from different cultures. As they usually retained a lot of attitudes and ways learned in their previous lifestyles, Paul had to deal with problems ranging from libertarianism to legalism. In two of his letters, he stated explicitly that love fulfils all God's law.

Writing to the Christians living at Galatia, he addressed their belief that they had to observe certain holy days, abstain from certain foods and adopt the sort of stringent religious code the Pharisees taught. But in explaining the freedom they had as Christians, Paul was quick to add that it should be a freedom to love others.[17]

> *Only do not use your freedom as an opportunity for the flesh [that is, to gratify physical, sensuous cravings], but through love serve one another. For the whole law is fulfilled in a single sentence: 'You shall love your neighbour as yourself'.*

In his letter to the Christians living at Rome, he described their obligation towards people who did not share their

---

[16] Some translations of Matthew 6:25 say 'take no thought' or 'do not be careful' but they go too far. Worry and anxiety are what Jesus prohibits, not sensible thought and responsible planning.

[17] Galatians 5:13-14.

faith.[18]

> *Owe no one anything, except to love each other, for the one who loves another has fulfilled the law. For the commandments, 'You shall not commit adultery, You shall not murder, You shall not steal, You shall not covet' and any other commandment, are summed up in this word: 'You shall love your neighbour as yourself'. Love does no wrong to a neighbour; therefore love is the fulfilling of the law.*

In the letter to his protégé, Timothy, in which he warned about the dangers of loving money, Paul sets out what is essentially the same paradigm for handling money that Jesus taught.[19]

> *Now there is great gain in godliness with contentment... But if we have food and clothing, with these we will be content. But those who desire to be rich fall into temptation, into a snare, into many senseless and harmful desires that plunge people into ruin and destruction. For the love of money is a root of all kinds of evils. It is through this craving that some have wandered away from the faith and pierced themselves with many pangs. But as for you, O man of God, flee these things. Pursue righteousness, godliness, faith, love, steadfastness, gentleness.*

This passage sets out three principles.

- Be content with food and clothing.
- Flee avarice and greed.
- Pursue righteousness, godliness, faith, love, steadfastness and gentleness.

---

[18] Romans 13:8-10.

[19] 1 Timothy 6:6-11.

As the Bible speaks of greater dangers in prosperity than austerity, it is important to remember that there is no sin in having money. There is nothing wrong with financial stability and physical comforts: they **are** God's blessing! And to be clear, Jesus never said or suggested that money was unimportant or irrelevant. But God has better things in mind for us.

Someone who came to realise this when he met Jesus was Zacchaeus, a corrupt tax collector who was prepared to change his allegiance from money to trust God unequivocally.[20] Although he had profited from the dubious practices of his profession, he undertook to give half of his possessions to the poor and to repay everyone he had cheated four times over. Zacchaeus was an accountant and knew this meant not only the end of his fortune but also, if he began to do his job honestly, the end of his comfortable lifestyle. He realised that money would not be nearly so important to him from then onwards.

Applying the Paradigm

The lifestyle Jesus described in the Sermon on the Mount was as radical then as it is now and the financial implications no less significant. He taught that the poor and those who suffer are blessed, the meek inherit the earth and the humble are exalted. The leaders are those who serve. We are to 'turn the other cheek' to those who abuse us and do good to our enemies. Our devotional and charitable actions done in secret are openly rewarded by God but the ones done 'to be seen' are (at best) of temporal advantage only. Money given to the poor buys incorruptible treasure in heaven but the treasures hoarded on earth are lost to theft and decay. It follows that Christians should not get and use money like everyone else. It is not just unnecessary but self-defeating!

---

[20] See Luke 19:2-10.

Before we consider the financial implications, it may be helpful if you take a few minutes to read the entire Sermon straight through (Matthew 5-7). It should only take about 20 minutes.

In the passage on plain speaking, Jesus advocated honesty in every situation because a system of socially acceptable deceit had built up around the Torah. On another occasion, he observed that if someone 'swore by the altar', their oath was not taken so seriously as if they swore by the gift they had sacrificed on the altar.[21] Today, we might hear someone saying, 'Let me be frank' or 'I'm going to level with you', suggesting, albeit implicitly, that they might not always be so truthful! It is a sad fact of life that people often say things they do not mean, knowing that they can get away with it.

When Jesus spoke about the 'wickedness' of unreasonable demands made by people, he was not talking about illegality but of taking advantage of people within the law, often from positions of political, commercial or social superiority.

- A slap on the cheek was a formal challenge, not the start of a brawl. It was like throwing down a gauntlet or glove in later generations or a solicitor's letter today. Government agencies, big business and rich people may threaten legal action to quash justified criticism or to force their will on people, knowing that the cost implications will often compel compliance.
- Being taken to court for our tunic was an example of harsh action by creditors. Today, this sort of thing happens because debt collection systems and civil court procedures are highly automated and poverty-related crime is routinely punished with financial penalties and fines.

---

[21] See Matthew 23:16-22.

- Going the extra mile was an example of inconvenient and sometimes unfair demands made by State officials. A Roman soldier in an occupied country could require a citizen to carry his baggage and equipment for one mile. In many countries today, officials expect bribes. But the problem is more widespread than that. We might be stopped by police officers or ticketed by parking attendants for minor, technical infringements with mitigating circumstances because they have their own performance targets to meet.

I am not trying to make a political point here but only giving commonplace examples of how financial considerations trump in most areas of life, even in modern democracies with developed human rights legislation and judicial systems. If public servants are tasked to meet performance targets, ones usually founded on financial imperatives, in order to keep their jobs and advance their careers, they will not think too deeply about the consequences of their decisions for others.

By telling us to love our enemies and those who persecute us, Jesus created an obligation towards all these people. This includes our colleagues who compete with us for pay rises and promotions and our business rivals who battle with us for market share. It continues even when their tactics are unscrupulous: manipulating statistics, for example, misrepresenting resources, circulating fake news and disrupting family life.

Although the ways we love our enemies will not be the same as how we love our friends, the obligation stands. We will not, for example, expect our friends to lie to us or about us and so caution is necessary with people who have chosen to be our enemies. But when a need is clear and genuine, we ought to respond to it kindly. Paul expands the point at the end of Romans 12.

> *Never avenge yourselves, but leave it to the wrath of God, for it is written, 'Vengeance is mine, I will repay, says the Lord'. To the contrary, 'if your enemy is hungry, feed him; if he is thirsty, give him something to drink; for by so doing you will heap burning coals on his head'. Do not be overcome by evil, but overcome evil with good.*

In explaining that we should do good works modestly and discretely, Jesus wanted us to value God's favour more than people's approval. This is especially important when we engage in a 'Christian' activity. If we keep bringing what we do to the attention of others, hoping they will support us financially, then we risk forfeiting God's favour, so that the very best we can hope for is people's money![22]

Work Parameters

When Jesus pointed to how magnificently God provides for birds and flowers, he was not implying that we could be just as passive as them. Rather, the ways God feeds and clothes his creatures that cannot work should give confidence to those who can.

When God apportioned the Promised Land among the twelve tribes of Israel, so the settlers could provide for themselves, the Law included requirements that formed the backdrop to Jesus' teaching about work and which remain valid for understanding the nature and function of work today.

- God gave the land for an inheritance: it was not for exploitation in the short or medium term by whoever owned it at the time but it had to be preserved for future generations. Production had to be sustainable.

[22] As it is not central to the paradigm, I explore fundraising and giving in an appendix.

- The people had a duty to care for their neighbours' property and welfare. This was demonstrated by the laws of restitution about straying cattle: *both* the damage they might do *and* the harm they might come to.
- The produce of the land was not for the exclusive benefit of the owners but available for the whole community. Fields could not be harvested to the edges or harvested twice, so that poor people could help themselves and not be chased away as scavengers.[23]

We should behave just as responsibly today. We should be just as concerned about those who come after us, just as mindful of neighbours and just as willing to use what we earn to help others, especially those who struggle to eat well and dress warmly. Even those who are our 'rivals'. This is the very least that is necessary to fulfil the fundamental command to love our neighbours as ourselves.

Nothing I have written should suggest that a business should not operate at a profit. Clearly, no bankrupt business can serve its community! But the need to trade at a profit should be in balance with other factors. Put positively, I think a business ceases to be capitalist when the following is true.

- It values the human contribution far above the financial one.
- It provides goods or services for the good of the community.
- It prices goods and services according to intrinsic worth, not for whatever price the market will bear

[23] Not only poor people but wild animals were also allowed to feed on this produce, so that this law made ecological as well as economic sense.

to yield the maximum profit.

- It competes for its market share by quality and honest advertising, without pretence or by disparaging others.
- It promotes itself, its goods and services, in a way that does not seek to manipulate the market.

If you think these are impossible ideals, then you may need to consider a new business model or perhaps a wholly new job and career path. There is more about this in the third appendix, *Business is Business*, which you may find helpful in thinking through fundamental Christian principles as they apply to business, to keep in sight God's expectations and people's rights.

Workplace Integrity

Traditionally, Christians have been exhorted by their pastors and teachers to be exemplary employees, following the directions to slaves and servants in Ephesians 6, Colossians 3-4 and 1 Peter 2. As a young Christian, I recall learning how my behaviour at work should be marked by honesty and integrity, fidelity and loyalty; by punctuality, truthfulness, diligence, quality of work and devotion to employers' interests. This is sound advice but I think we need to say more today.

Although employees are not implicated in everything their employers do, and although they should not constantly be second-guessing and challenging their employers' policies and procedures, there is a line which, if crossed, will take them outside God's favour. It might not be easy to know where that line is in any particular situation, as one suspect action does not necessarily indicate duplicity or dishonesty as a business norm. But Christians should not take it for granted that shades of deception is simply the way we now live.

- Should we earn money in ways that fail to make a positive contribution to society, making life better for people?
- Should we take part in business activity that relies on exaggerating goods and services, like so much marketing, advertising and sales talk do?
- Should we do anything to exploit other people's misfortune, like increasing prices in times of shortage or difficulty or tragedy?
- Should we manipulate data (accounts, statistics and projections) for commercial or political expediency?
- Should we embellish actual performance or attainable potential in order to get customers, clients or credit?
- Should we use psychological tactics to put emotional pressure on people to spend or borrow needlessly?
- Should we try to deceive people, perhaps by claiming to be following up reports or surveys, when we call them to sell goods and services?
- Should we try to create an illusion of authority we do not have?
- Should we rely on misdirection and convenient irrelevancies to evade responsibility for errors and poor service?
- Should we be involved with anything dubious or dishonest that makes it more difficult for a business rival to do well?

I need to conclude this list by heading off a possible misunderstanding. At a church where I was explaining to some cell group leaders what I would later teach about money, I was suddenly interrupted by one who said something like this. 'We have in our groups people working in banking and credit and before your talk starts we need to make it clear that you are not getting at them personally.'

The person could not identify anything I had said to suggest that I was being critical of Christians in that type of work but I have learned that it is best to anticipate that inference. I should therefore be clear that the world needs good bankers, accountants, credit controllers, sales executives, debt collectors and enforcement officers every bit as much as it needs good doctors, teachers, social workers, lawyers, politicians, truck drivers and plumbers. But all Christians who really want to live as Jesus' followers should think seriously about whether they are able to do the particular job expected of them *and* remain true to what Jesus taught.

Returning to our behaviour, we should think seriously about the extent to which we use typical workplace tactics to secure jobs and promotions.

- Do we talk or write about ourselves in interviews and on social media using overblown adjectives to describe our personalities, skills and achievements?
- Do we exaggerate our abilities and experience on CVs and job applications?
- When pursuing pay rises and promotions, do we start by asking for more than we want, and so dissemble and begin to haggle, rather than asking for what we want honestly, straightforwardly and sincerely?
- Do we allow colleagues to fail in order to gain a career advantage?

Lifestyle Challenges

The decisions that we make about how we use money are tied up with how we feel about ourselves, how we want others to feel about us, who we respect and who we wish to please. As it is often easier to observe what we do than how we think, we should examine how we use money day by day. But this scrutiny is possible only when we track every penny we spend.

When I began teaching personal finance, I soon discovered how very difficult it is to persuade people to keep a spending diary. While it is a bother, it seems that the greater problem is that they are afraid of what they might discover about themselves. But the self-awareness that comes by tracking our spending is worth the effort and any emotional discomfort.

It is necessary to record everything – *every single thing* – that we buy or pay for. Every direct debit and standing order; every card and cash purchase. Every fuel bill, insurance premium, supermarket trip, mobile top-up, music download, movie, in-game purchase, bus ride, magazine, snack, sweet and drink. Every pound spent on petrol, oil, road tax and insurance; every visit to the car wash. Every dollar dropped in a church collection or charity box.

Record each thing you pay for in a small notebook as you go because it is easy to forget something by the end of a day.

After a week, start to study what you have bought. It may surprise you. It will show your priorities and weaknesses; it will help you see whether you really are the person you think you are. Over a longer period, work in other spending, like rent, mortgage and household bills to see how much of your total spending is essential and what goes on non-essentials such as leisure and entertainment.[24] And how much you give to help people less fortunate than you.

These questions may help you probe beneath the lifestyle you are used to and which may seem modest compared to your neighbours and work colleagues.

- Do we, perhaps unconsciously, evaluate people by their home, car, clothes, possessions or income?
- Do we instinctively compare what we own to what others have?
- Are we anxious for our children to have the same status symbols and lifestyle accessories as their friends?
- Are we intuitively influenced by the lifestyles portrayed on television and in newspapers and magazines?
- Do we feel that we may be missing out on opportunities or bargains?
- Do we feel we have little choice but to spend money to maintain a lifestyle that matches our friends, neighbours or work colleagues?
- What are our fashion statements? These are more than just wearing a style of clothes that we are comfortable in. A fashion statement is to draw attention to ourselves and say something about us: a particular hairstyle, perhaps, or a 'trademark' hat or other fashion accessory that we wear in all weathers, indoors and out.

---

[24] Leisure activities and entertainment are not unimportant but they are secondary to the things we need to survive: food, clothing, housing, taxes, medical care, travel to and from work and the other inescapable costs of living in a modern society.

- Does advertising create in us a desire for possessions and experiences (leisure activities, entertainments and holidays) that feels almost irresistible?
- Do sales staff easily talk us into upgrading to more expensive alternatives or buying accessories we had not previously thought we wanted?
- Do we keep finding ourselves justifying our extravagance? *It's my treat to myself. I deserve it. I'm worth it.*
- Do we buy things sold by advertising that generates fear? The latest gadgets that are less likely to break down or the latest security systems for our homes, cars and computers? Or excessive insurance and investments, in the hope they insulate us against unlikely catastrophe?
- Do we buy goods and services in an effort to become better people or better liked? Things we hope will make us more capable, reliable, relaxed or happy?
- Are we addicted to things and experiences, like alcohol, fast food, chocolate, tobacco, shopping, exercise, gambling, music, movies and computer games?

Finally, consider this prayer of Agur, a man who collected wise sayings.[25]

> *Two things I ask of you; deny them not to me before I die: Remove far from me falsehood and lying give me neither poverty nor riches; feed me with the food that is needful for me, lest I be full and deny you and say, 'Who is the LORD?' or lest I be poor*

[25] Proverbs 30:7-9.

and steal and profane the name of my God.

Agur knew when he was well off, unlike Lucifer, Eve, Nebuchadnezzar and most of us. He saw the dangers in wealth as well as the evils of poverty. The phrase 'feed me with the food that is needful for me' can be translated many ways. The Hebrew word translated food literally means bread and what is needful refers to our daily portion. That is the meaning behind the phrase, 'Give us this day our daily bread', in the prayer that Jesus taught his disciples. I think it fair to say that if we cannot with sincerity pray Agur's prayer, we should not join in Jesus' prayer!

The Limitations of Liberty

Ask yourself how your spending helps you live as a Christian. This was something that Paul put to the Christians in Corinth. They were very different to the Christians in Galatia, whose lives were controlled by restrictive rules and regulations. In Corinth, for the most part, the Christians thought they could live very much like everyone else in the city.

Life in Corinth was not too different from our consumer society. It was a Greek port on an important trade route across the Roman Empire. It had a reputation for high-minded philosophy, extravagance, sexual immorality and financial corruption. And there was a saying in the Empire, 'Do it like a Corinthian!', which meant that the people there knew how to party.

The Christians there knew they were saved by God's grace, so that nothing could separate them from Jesus Christ's love. But they rationalised from this assurance that all things were 'lawful' for them to enjoy. Paul explained that although all things might be allowed, they should question whether somethings worked to their detriment. His criteria can be summarised by putting together his comments in I Corinthians 6:12 & 10:23.

> *All things are lawful for me, but not all things are helpful. All things are lawful for me, but I will not be enslaved by anything... All things are lawful, but not all things build up.*

With this in mind, challenge yourself with these three questions.

- Is what I buy helpful?
- Could I be addicted to what I buy?
- Is my spending constructive?

For most of us, there is more to these questions than we think. The idea behind the word 'helpful' refers to what actively moves us forward. Other translations say expedient, beneficial or profitable. It means that we should reject anything that does not advance us towards Christian maturity: any fashions, for example, or gadgets, magazines, music, movies, nights out and holidays. Anything.

To be enslaved by something is to be under its power: to be addicted to it. Not all addictions are harmful but they all keep us spending. More importantly, some can change us by stimulating our senses and staining our imagination.

- Do we, for example, enjoy novels or movies that include gratuitous violence and strong language or that applaud vanity, greed or sexual betrayal?
- In computer games and role-play, do we imitate the sort of aggression and violence we would not want to commit in real life? Do we exercise by simulating violence?
- Does the music we enjoy arouse carnal feelings or do we get pleasure from dance moves that mimic sensual behaviour?

Finally, do we invest our personality, time and money in people and projects that build up relationships and lead people to see the truth about Jesus? In 1 Corinthians 10,

Paul describes principles of Christian behaviour when shopping and accepting hospitality. He sums up by saying that we should do everything to the glory of God, not seeking our own advantage but the advantage of others, 'that they may be saved'. Does our spending contribute to this?

Paul addressed a similar situation in his letter to the Christians living at Rome where the behaviour of some was what Paul called 'a stumbling block' for others. Following the passages I mentioned earlier, he went on to explain how members of the Christian community should treat each other. He knew that there were quarrels between those who abstained from certain foods and observed certain holy days and those who did neither. He explained that while each person should be fully convinced about what to do they should not judge each other. So far so good. But then he added something easily misunderstood.[26]

> *Therefore let us not pass judgment on one another any longer, but rather decide never to put a stumbling block or hindrance in the way of a brother... For if your brother is grieved by what you eat, you are no longer walking in love...*
>
> *Do not, for the sake of food, destroy the work of God. Everything is indeed clean, but it is wrong for anyone to make another stumble by what he eats. It is good not to eat meat or drink wine or do anything that causes your brother to stumble...*

Paul was not saying that another Christian's opinion should dictate our behaviour. If he had meant that, we should all be subject to the most extreme legalists who call themselves Christian! What he meant was that we should be concerned about the impact of our opinions and

---

[26] Romans 14:13-23.

choices on the faith of others: not whether it offends their theological sensitivities but whether it genuinely causes them difficulties and, perhaps, entices them to act contrary to what they firmly believe is right.

Paul's point was that we should judge ourselves, not others, but the standard we use to judge ourselves is the welfare of others. One of our greatest freedoms as Christians is the freedom to abandon our rights for the benefit of others. Paul summed up the whole issue by appealing for behaviour that produces peace and mutual edification. This is loving our neighbour as we love ourselves.

It is important not to ignore what we learn about ourselves as we consider our lifestyles and the ways we get and use money. To use the analogy from James' letter, we should not be like people who look intently at themselves in a mirror and then forget what they saw. If we can see lifestyle choices inconsistent with what Jesus taught, we need to change. If we do not, how can we expect people to take seriously anything we say that we believe about Jesus?

The Misunderstood Manager

Jesus' parables illustrate the lifestyle he described in the Sermon on the Mount but, as we have grown up with capitalism, we may misunderstand the financial aspects. The parable of the dishonest manager (or unjust steward) is probably the most misunderstood.[27]

> *There was a rich man who had a manager, and charges were brought to him that this man was wasting his possessions. And he called him and said to him, 'What is this that I hear about you? Turn in the account of your management, for you can no longer be manager.' And the manager said*

[27] Luke 16:1-8.

> *to himself, 'What shall I do, since my master is taking the management away from me? I am not strong enough to dig, and I am ashamed to beg. I have decided what to do, so that when I am removed from management, people may receive me into their houses.' So, summoning his master's debtors one by one, he said to the first, 'How much do you owe my master?' He said, 'A hundred measures of oil.' He said to him, 'Take your bill, and sit down quickly and write fifty.' Then he said to another, 'And how much do you owe?' He said, 'A hundred measures of wheat.' He said to him, 'Take your bill, and write eighty.' The master commended the dishonest manager for his shrewdness. For the sons of this world are more shrewd in dealing with their own generation than the sons of light.*

In my experience, three mistakes are common.

- That Jesus called the manager dishonest because he wasted his master's goods.
- That the manager was dishonest because he reduced the debts owed by the creditors.
- That Jesus commended the manager's dishonesty as shrewdness.

There is no reason to suppose that the dishonest manager was guilty of theft, fraud or any 'serious' dishonesty. If he had been, his master would not have trusted him to make up the accounts but immediately put him in prison until everything was repaid! He was, however, lazy to the point of incompetence, because he had to ask the debtors how much they owed. I expect the allegation that he wasted his master's goods means that he behaved like many managers who leverage their position. Putting it in modern terms, he exaggerated the hours he worked, took undue advantage of his expense account, manipulated performance targets and generally enjoyed the perks of his job rather more than was reasonable. He may have been like Judas Iscariot, who used his position as treasurer of the group that travelled with Jesus to steal from their common funds.[28] He may have been like the 'wicked' servant Jesus described at the end of Matthew 24, who wasted his time socialising with drunkards.

The manager was not dishonest for cutting the debts owed to his master because that was within his delegated authority. Actually, it was the right thing to do. The debtors were probably the master's tenants who owed rent, although they may have been customers who owed payment for goods. The manager was responsible for the master's business and, consequently, he was responsible for the welfare of not just the tenants and others who did business with his master but also their families. Making the reductions was therefore the responsible social action: the rich creditor who did not need the money reduced the amounts owed by poor people who did.

Why, then, was the manager dishonest? It was because he acted selfishly. He moved beyond wasting his master's goods to bartering them for personal gain, to secure his own future. If a bank executive today wrote off a debt on compassionate grounds, we would think it a good use of

---

[28] This allegation appears in John 12:6 but I have heard many preachers doubt that it was true. It was, they say, added later in order to discredit Judas even more than for betraying Jesus. If that were the case, it would have been a pointlessly superfluous invention! But not only do I take the allegation seriously, it seems to me to be entirely consistent with what we know of Judas. And still more likely if the theory is correct that he had previously been the manager of a rich man's estate, and so was well known to the Jerusalem elite, which is why he was trusted by the chief priests to betray Jesus. In fact, I would not be surprised to learn that Judas was the model for the dishonest manager in the parable.

the executive's discretion; if, however, we learn that he or she expected a personal benefit in return, we would question his or her integrity.

Jesus said that the dishonest manager was commended by his master for his shrewdness. But, crucially, Jesus did not commend the manager.[29] All Jesus said was that the master commended his manager. And then he explained the master's rationale like this. 'The sons of this world are more shrewd in dealing with their own generation than the sons of light.' In other words, people living according to the ways of society will do what everyone else does, even when it is illegal, when it is in their own self-interest. But, by contrast, the children of light, Christians, are not so pragmatic about living the way that Jesus described. We should not therefore conclude that Jesus wants us to be as selfishly pragmatic as the dishonest manager!

On another occasion, Jesus told a parable about an unjust judge to encourage his disciples to persevere in prayer. The judge did not fear God or respect people but he gave justice to an aggrieved widow when her persistent badgering began to annoy him. Was Jesus saying that God is like that judge? Or did Jesus want us to know how just and loving God is in comparison to the unjust judge?[30]

---

[29] The Greek word Jesus used for master is sometimes used for God and so some scholars believe that Jesus meant to say that God commended the dishonest manager. I find it very difficult to believe that was Jesus' intent.

[30] See Luke 18:1-8. I am dismayed when I hear pastors and teachers say we have to persist with our prayers as the widow had to pester the judge. While Christians are encouraged to 'be constant in prayer', to quote Paul in Romans 12, it means praying generally and does not imply that God has to be harassed into giving us the good things we desire. When he does withhold something, his reason is not usually hard to discover: see, for example, James 4:3.

Equally, Jesus does not want us to be like the selfish, dishonest manager. He does not, for example, want us to be good to our business rivals and work colleagues only because we want something back. He wants us to do the right thing, right according to the ways of God that he taught, and to do it cheerfully, simply because it is the right thing to do. Even when money is involved. Even if it is to our material disadvantage.

Jesus went on to say that we should make friends for ourselves by means of unrighteous mammon, and so opened up for us an entirely new destiny.

Making Friends

The full significance of money will only become apparent after we have died. In the Sermon on the Mount, Jesus spoke about using money to accumulate treasure in heaven and it is what he told the rich young ruler to do.[31] He elaborated on this as he explained the parable of dishonest manager.[32]

> *I tell you, make friends for yourselves by means of unrighteous wealth, so that when it fails they may receive you into the eternal dwellings. One who is faithful in a very little is also faithful in much, and one who is dishonest in a very little is also dishonest in much. If then you have not been faithful in the unrighteous wealth, who will entrust to you the true riches? And if you have not been faithful in that which is another's, who will give you that which is your own? No servant can serve two masters, for either he will hate the one and love the other, or he will be devoted to the one and*

---

[31] Compare, for example, Matthew 6:19-21 & Mark 10:21. I will examine the rich young ruler's meeting with Jesus later.

[32] Luke 16:9-13.

> *despise the other. You cannot serve God and money.*

If you look up this passage in a printed copy of an ESV Bible, you will see that the first sentence concludes the previous paragraph, rather than begin this paragraph. The original books that make up the Bible were not arranged in paragraphs and translators have to use their best judgement to know where to insert paragraph breaks. These are usually helpful but in this case I think it obscures what Jesus meant about making friends 'by means of unrighteous wealth'. Also, if the phrase, 'unrighteous wealth' were translated literally, it would read 'unrighteous mammon'. This is important because, as I hope I have already made clear, wealth is not necessarily unrighteous but mammon, the power of money, is always unrighteous, because it controls and corrupts. Also, the word translated 'money' at the end of the passage should, if also translated literally, be 'mammon'. We can, therefore, fairly summarise Jesus' view by picking out the three references to mammon, like this.

> *I tell you, make friends for yourselves by means of unrighteous mammon... If then you have not been faithful in the unrighteous mammon, who will entrust to you the true riches? ...You cannot serve God and mammon.*

Or we can put it like this.

- Use mammon to make friends for eternity.
- Our faithfulness using mammon is both training for and a test of our worthiness to handle greater responsibility.
- Do not try to serve both God and mammon.

We need to remember that Jesus was talking to his disciples. He would later talk to his critics, the Pharisees who were listening and would mock him, but Luke makes it clear that these words were for the people already committed to him. Like them, we are to do good with the proceeds of mammon but we are not to serve mammon, as if accumulating more would be our opportunity to do even more good. That would be like thinking we should sin more in order to experience even more forgiveness!

I must digress for a moment to expand that point because it is, in my experience, underestimated by Christians who rationalise that getting rich will enable them to finance God's work. In the 4th Century, Evagrios the Solitary warned that the desire for wealth for giving to the poor is 'another trick of the evil one'. In the 18th Century, Charles Finney spoke to Christians about the dangers of 'conforming to the world' in business practice in order to make money that could be used to spread the Gospel. 'A holy church', he said, 'that would act on the principles of the Gospel, would spread the Gospel faster than all the money that ever was in New York, or ever will be.'

But while we should not seek to use the power of money, it is a fact of life that we all benefit from it: at least, to some degree. It is impossible not to. It would, for example, be impossible for us to comply with Augustine's view that no part of our giving should include the proceeds of interest, because charging interest has become so integrated into our way of life that it is unavoidable. I once read a book that claimed that every US dollar bill had been used in at least one illegal drug deal; similarly, we have no way of knowing if the money in our bank accounts was ever the proceeds of crime or profit made by exploiting people. But while we should not be totally indifferent to where our money comes from, we cannot worry about it unduly. After all, it is just data in computer systems and has not really 'come' from anywhere! What matters is that we use what we have to make friends for eternity.

When Jesus referred to what is 'very little', he was not talking about a small amount of money but the relative unimportance of mammon, the power of money. Although money may seem to be the supreme influence in the world, Jesus saw it for what it is. By contrast, the 'much' that he mentioned is 'true riches', or spiritual wealth. That really is important, both in this world and throughout eternity.

Jesus was not saying that integrity in the little things matters. That is true but he was making a very different point. He was saying that people who cannot handle faithfully the power of money cannot be trusted with true power: the spiritual riches, the heavenly treasure. The material wealth we enjoy now is not ours to keep but belongs to 'another', to God. That is why we cannot take it with us when we die. But the ways we manage it affects our destiny after we die: that is why we cannot serve both the power of money and God! Zacchaeus, the reformed tax collector, is an example of someone who made good use of the money he had accumulated dishonestly: he gave half to the poor and repaid everyone he had cheated four times. I sometimes wonder how he went on to serve God for the rest of his life.

Time & Eternity

In two of his parables, Jesus talked about the responsibility of servants while their masters are away.[33]

---

[33] See Matthew 25:14-30 & Luke 19:12-27. I have heard Christians say that by these parables Jesus ended the prohibition on interest because the masters told their unworthy servants that, rather than hide their money in the ground, they should have banked it and got the interest. We should remember, however, that the masters were telling the servants what they should have done had they thought their masters to be severe, hard, austere men who expected to reap what they had not sown. The implication is that only those sorts of people expect

The masters give resources to their servants and, on their return, reward those servants with varying degrees of responsibility, based on how they handled those resources during their absence. The parables therefore indicate our responsibility as Christians here and now, using the resources that God entrusts to us, and the reward that awaits us in the future. The choice was, and still is, between living like most people in society, for our own advantage in the here and now, and living the sort of life Jesus described – one focused on eternity and built on the foundation of loving God with our entire being and loving our neighbour as ourselves.

But I must again digress, to avoid the possibility of a serious misunderstanding about treasure in heaven and the eternal reward that Paul and the other New Testament authors wrote about. While Peter explained that we have kept for us in heaven 'an inheritance that is imperishable, undefiled, and unfading', Paul explained how we can lose ours by indulging selfish desires, such as greed and covetousness. No heir to an earthly title or fortune can earn their inheritance but they can renounce it or forfeit it; likewise, we cannot earn our heavenly inheritance but we can lose it.[34]

The Pharisees who heard Jesus talking to his disciples jeered him. They were, as Luke tells us, lovers of money. Perhaps they saw themselves as serving both God and money; perhaps, if we had asked them, they would have said that God was more important to them than money. But, inevitably, their devotion was to money. Jesus accused them of spiritual adultery, likening them to those

---

interest, which I expect is why the literal meaning of usury is to sting like a serpent.

[34] Compare, for example, 1 Corinthians 9:24-25, Ephesians 5:4, 2 Timothy 4:8, James 1:12 & 1 Peter 1:4; see also what Jesus promises to the conquerors, or overcomers, in Revelation 2-3.

who divorce their wives to marry someone else. And then he told them a parable about an unnamed rich man who did not use 'unrighteous mammon' to make friends for eternity by caring for the poor sick man named Lazarus lying at the gate to his home.

I include myself when I say that the example of these Pharisees should serve as our wake up call.

- Are we regular at church services? So were these Pharisees.
- Do we study the Scriptures? So did these Pharisees.
- Are we faithful witnesses? These Pharisees could be easily recognized by their distinctive clothes and religious habits. And the best seats in the synagogues were reserved for them.
- Do we tithe? These Pharisees even tithed the herbs and spices they grew!
- Do we make money legally? So did these Pharisees. But within the law, they behaved no more scrupulously than anyone else and exploited vulnerable people.
- Are we assured of a welcome into heaven? These Pharisees thought they were!

Deliberate Choices

Many of Jesus' parables illustrate ways to handle money contrary to the norms of capitalism and consumerism. In the parable of the vineyard workers, those hired at 6am, 9am, noon and 3pm are all paid the same wage.[35] There is a clear spiritual application but, equally, a practical one. Their employer had promised to pay each worker 'whatever is right' and so paid them all the daily living

---

[35] See Matthew 20:1-16.

wage. This allowed all the workers and their families to eat that day! Many people, then and now, cannot see how this can be right or fair but the landowner's generosity was neither arbitrary nor profligate. By ensuring the welfare of all the workers and their families, he acted for the greater good of the whole community.

By contrast, the rich farmer that Jesus described in another parable was foolish when he decided to hoard his abundant harvest.[36] He had been dependent on God for it and did not have an exclusive right to it. He should have thought about the needs of his workers, their families and the wider community. This is not to suggest that he should have given it away, for it would have been right for him to have sold it at a fair price, but he was wrong to hoard it to fund his own ease.

In the story of the rich man and Lazarus, the rich man did not mistreat or abuse Lazarus. He may even have allowed his servants to give Lazarus left over food and unwanted clothing. But he failed to love his neighbour, the homeless, sick man lying at his gate, as he loved himself. And having failed to make friends for eternity, he found himself isolated and alone.[37]

This is not reading too much into the parables. They were stories of daily life, not fairy tales, crafted to help people understand spiritual truths, and therefore had to mirror Jesus' understanding of how life should be lived.

In Acts 2, we read how the first Christians lived. As well as being devoted to teaching and the sacraments, and seeing signs and wonders, and leading people to faith in Jesus, they 'had all things in common [and] were selling

---

[36] See Luke 12:16-21.

[37] See Luke 16:19-31. The rich man also seemed to have had little regard for the welfare of his own servants, if the observation that he 'feasted sumptuously *every* day' implies they were not allowed a day off on the Sabbath.

their possessions and belongings and distributing the proceeds to all, as any had need'. They were not living in a commune and were by no means communists, because they still owned their own property, but these things no longer held the same importance for them. People were far more important.

The Desert Fathers were Christians who responded to the 'Christianisation' of the Roman Empire during the 3rd Century by retreating into the hard isolation of the desert. While I cannot endorse everything they did and said, their discipleship was not compromised by financial concerns. 'When buying or selling you can hardly avoid sin', one of them wrote. 'So, in either case, be sure you lose a little in the transaction. Do not haggle about the price for love of gain, and so indulge in actions harmful to the soul – quarrelling, lying, shifting your ground and so on – thus bringing our way of life into disrepute.'

The hermits made things they could sell at market, in order to get the money they needed to buy food and other supplies. One of them is remembered because he sold what he made to the people who most needed it, for whatever price they could afford, and bought what he needed from those who most needed his custom, for whatever price they asked.

John Woolman (1720-1772) was a remarkable American who first earned his living running a store and then, in order to simplify his lifestyle, worked as a tailor. His Journal is full of useful insights that can help us reflect on life today, including these two.

> *It had been my general practice to buy and sell things really useful. Things that served chiefly to please the vain mind in people, I was not easy to trade in; seldom did it; and whenever I did I found it weaken me as a Christian...*

> *In merchandise it is the custom where I lived to sell chiefly on credit, and poor people often get in debt;*

> *when payment is expected, not having wherewith to pay, their creditors often sue for it at law. Having frequently observed occurrences of this kind, I found it good for me to advise poor people to take such goods as were most useful, and not costly.*

Woolman also earned money helping people make their wills but he refused to work for people who owned slaves, except in rare cases when he thought his refusal might cause undue hardship to the family. When he travelled, he wanted to minimise any contribution he might make to the exploitation of the child labour relied on by the travel companies. That is why he refused a ship's cabin on his voyage to England and then walked the 200 miles from London to York, rather than ride in stagecoaches.

We might think that Woolman was too fastidious, too strenuous in his wish not to exploit others. Perhaps he was. But his and our paramount concern is to live in a way that fulfils our divine obligation to love God and to love our neighbours as ourselves. The degree to which we can do this will depend on the extent to which we trust God more than money.

3: A WONDERFUL POTENTIAL

It seems to me to be so much humbug to be praying as we are praying, to be waiting as we are waiting, if we ourselves are not rightly related to God.

Comment of a young man at a prayer meeting for revival in the Hebrides, 1950.

The Potential for Revival

The issues for Christians who are concerned about trends in our society tend to be the reverse of what worries people with a social conscience who profess no faith. Christians are often vocal about sexual issues. People who espouse no particular Christian faith tend to accept these social developments but abhor the ruthless pursuit of profit, the subversive effects of marketing and the economic equalities that pay bankers very much more than nurses and teachers. One effect of this is to make Christians appear greedy for gain, indifferent to hardship and intolerant of personal freedoms. This is, as I well know, a generalisation that, like all generalisations, is unfair. But it is a major factor in why the Christian faith, and even Christ Jesus himself, appear irrelevant to many people in the world today.

I am not suggesting that sexual issues are unimportant, only that they have distracted many Christians from something of equal importance. Arguably, of greater importance, given the priority Jesus placed on our attitude to money and how we use it and its effect on our relationship with God and with each other.

In the earlier part of this book, I expressed the hope that readers who profess no Christian faith would give a fair hearing to what Jesus said about money. Now, my hope is that Christian readers will give serious attention to it. And to the current widespread disinterest in, and sometimes hostility towards, Christianity. And to address these issues in the only way that Christians have ever successfully addressed such challenges in the past. By repentance and revival.

I must explain that this is a chapter that I never thought I could write because I have no personal experience of revival. But during the 50 years that I have been reading about revivals, I have realised that no community will experience it unless at least one local church there experiences it first. And that no church will experience revival unless some of the Christians there are serious about repentance. And, moreover, after many years teaching personal finance to Christians, I have become convinced that the attitude of Christians today towards mammon, the power of money, is the single greatest hindrance to revival in our consumer society.

Churches that readily comment on marriage breakdown, sex outside marriage, homosexual and transgender issues seem to have nothing to say about avarice, covetousness or greed. The most I hear about financial sin is that we must be honest. That is obviously true! But that approach is wholly inadequate in a consumer society: after all, even Ebenezer Scrooge always was an honest businessman![38]

[38] Scrooge, 'a grasping, covetous old man', is the central character in *A Christmas Carol*, Charles Dickens' most famous novel published in 1843.

It would be impossible for me to explain how my thinking about this has developed, or who among the many authors I have read is responsible for many of the insights that follow. As I said, I did not expect to write about this and so did not keep notes. But I can say that I have been influenced most by Jonathan Edwards (1703-1758), Charles Finney (1792-1875) and J Edwin Orr (1912-1987). I have read many accounts of the Welsh Revival of 1904-1906, including the newspaper cuttings from the time preserved by G Campbell Morgan in his scrapbooks. Duncan Campbell's accounts of the Hebrides Revival of 1949-1950 have been both fascinating and helpful. Most recently, I have learned about the East African Revival that ran from the 1930s into the 1960s, mainly from the first-hand record left by Dr J E 'Joe' Church in his book, *Quest for the Highest*, and by the audio recordings left by him, William Nagenda, Festo Kivengere and others who were involved in the Revival when they spoke about it during their visits to the UK.[39]

The Toronto Blessing

My only experience of anything like revival was during the Toronto Blessing, a global renewal movement that began in 1994. The name was coined by the British newspaper, *The Daily Telegraph*, when it reported how the sort of spiritual experiences at a church in Toronto had spread to London churches. Although the origins of the 'Blessing' were more diverse, Toronto Airport Fellowship became a place of pilgrimage for Christians from around the world.

I have no doubt that the Toronto Blessing was genuine spiritual renewal. I was among those blessed. It

[39] Recordings of many of these messages are available for free download from the website, *Sermons of Grace*. It can be found at www.sermonsofgrace.org

transformed churches around the world in ways that endure today, 25 years later. It continued many of the innovations begun 30 years before with the revival known as the Jesus Revolution, because of the number of hippies touched. But having said that, I understood the concerns voiced by people who thought the Toronto Blessing was (at best) religious emotionalism or (at worst) demonic. Immediate causes of concern were the way that people fell to the floor when they 'came under the power of the Holy Spirit', the extensive 'laughing in the Spirit' and the animal noises heard during services.

In the longer term, the Blessing seemed to facilitate a growing irreverence among some Christians. All through history, there have been devout and gifted preachers with a fine sense of humour. But what began as a welcome casualness, so that 'church' became more accessible to groups of people who would previously have found the traditional ways too stuffy and stifling to be able grasp the truths behind them, sometimes evolved into dangerous flippancy. Some preachers even began referring to the Triune God as Father, Son and Holy Bam-Bam, because of how people fell down – 'slayed in the spirit', they said – when prayed for.

The Toronto Blessing was therefore a mixed blessing. It was also, I believe, a time of unfulfilled potential. With few exceptions, communities were not touched by the revival of faith in churches. I think the main reason for this was insufficient attention given to repentance. Instead, it seemed to me, most Christians thought revival would come if they prayed longer and worshipped louder.

To be fair to those Christians – and for a long while, I was among them – they heard many prophecies that promised just that. I remember hearing how, as clouds gather up warm moisture over the oceans and then release it as rain over dry ground, so our prayers and praises ascend from churches and descend as revival on communities. In as much as I am in a position to evaluate such prophecies, at least some had a ring of truth. But I think most Christians failed to grasp that we can only pray and praise with what the Bible calls clean hands and pure hearts (see Psalm 24). That is, after we have repented and put our own lives right in God's sight.

As I will describe later, when in 1904 Christians in Wales thought that God wanted to send revival there, they turned to him in renewed personal repentance. Evan Roberts famously called on them to turn not just from obvious sin but from anything doubtful in their lives. Fifty years later, revival began on the Scottish island of Lewis when the church leaders called their congregations to repentance. A turning point came at a prayer meeting for those leaders when a young man prayed the words that are so important to the theme of this book that I put them at the front: 'It seems to me to be so much humbug to be praying [for revival] as we are praying, to be waiting as we are waiting, if we ourselves are not rightly related to God.' Humbug is frivolous or pretentious talk.

Those words illustrate our situation as much as what was happening then. The Christians on Lewis were, like many of us living now in consumer societies around the world, relatively prosperous. They were neither rich nor poor according to the standards of the time but they lived comfortably. Employment levels were high; delinquency and crime rates low. Their daily round of life was stable and pleasant. But unbelievers were unmoved by the Gospel message; lukewarm believers were content because, on the surface, life seemed so very normal and ordinary. As it does to us today.

The more I have learned about the Toronto Blessing, the more remarkable it seemed that Christians failed to seize on the potential for revival. Especially in the UK. A desire for spiritual renewal had been growing during the 1980s and given added incentive in October 1990, when

John Wimber and a team from Vineyard churches in America held one of their *Holiness Unto the Lord* conferences in London. About 800 people attended, mostly pastors and teachers, and personal holiness was a priority. In the weeks before, there was a significant prophetic indication that seeds of revival would be sown there. But, looking back, it seems to me that prophecy eclipsed everything. While holiness was indeed preached, and another prophetic insight said how 'God wants to take his church back', nothing much seemed to happen as a result. I was aware of Christians constantly discussing and reassessing the prophecies but heard nothing about the call to holiness.

On reflection, perhaps too much was said at the conference about how Christians have imputed righteousness – that is, how God's righteousness and holiness is 'credited' to us when we become Christian – and not enough about the need to proactively pursue righteous living – to make right choices and develop right attitudes consistent with Jesus' teaching. It is a distinction that I did not really understand for a long time.[40]

As the Toronto Blessing gained momentum, it seemed like most Christians thought that God was inviting them to simply enjoy spiritual refreshment. In fact, one of the first church leaders from the UK to visit Toronto went because, 'I've never been one to pass up on a good party'. Fair enough. After all, that refreshment was badly needed! But, generally, we got excited about prayer ministry, speaking in tongues, prophecy, prayers for healing, words

[40] As Paul begins to explain from the start of Romans 4, our faith is 'counted' to us as righteousness. But this is only the start of 'right' living. I invite you to put aside time to meditate on Colossians 3:1-17. Some of behaviour and attitudes that Paul describes may instinctively develop in us, a natural consequence of our faith, but most will require determined effort on our part.

of knowledge and did not see a need to press on from that to proactively pursue lifestyle holiness. The spiritual refreshment that should have been a catalyst was, instead, our 'fix'.

The Necessity of Life

I think the first revival that gripped my imagination revolved around the ministry of William Haslam in Cornwall during the 1850s. Haslam came to be known as the parson converted by his own sermon. He was a High Church Anglican, a follower of the Tractarian Movement that had begun in 1833 at Oxford University, when John Henry Newman (later, Cardinal Newman) published the first of the *Tracts for our Times*. This Movement was a reaction against the 'evangelical' form of Christianity that prevailed in the Church of England at the time: a lifeless, faithless, empty, largely irrelevant religion.

Tractarianism had a 'high' view of both ancient church practice and the Bible. It was a form of Christianity that had substance: doctrines to believe and devotions to fulfil. It was no wonder that Haslam adopted its liturgies and preached its sermons. But as sincere as he was in his commitment, as reverently as he sought to perform his duties, and as concerned as he was for the welfare of his parishioners, Haslam found his ministry inadequate and unsatisfactory.

He described it as a rope made of sand that looked good until you tried to pull on it! In time, he came to see that he had been, as he described it, 'building from the top'. When work was ready to begin on a new church building outside Truro, a woman asked Haslam if he was going to begin with the steeple. It was a strange question! No, he replied. Obviously, he would begin with the foundation. He later realised that she was pointing out the futility of trying to promote spiritual lifestyle where there was no spiritual life to build it on.

Although most of Haslam's congregation were themselves 'content with dry, dead, empty husks and formal ceremonies', he feared for his own spiritual wellbeing. One bright Sunday morning in October 1851, he woke up feeling so unwell and unfit to conduct the services that he was about to cancel them when the church bells rang to summon the congregation. As the church began to fill, Haslam roused himself.

He found the service very soothing and the Bible readings seemed to speak to him especially. The hymns greatly comforted him. And so he went into the pulpit to speak briefly using the text 'What think ye of Christ?' (Matthew 22:42). As he spoke, he came to see more clearly how Jesus, the Son of God, came to save and deliver sinners from the power of sin and the devil. And he saw that the Pharisees had been so taken up with themselves, their services and sacrifices, that they could not see Jesus as he was, even though he was there demonstrating his divinity.

When Haslam explained to his congregation that the trouble with the Pharisees was that they did not believe that Jesus was the Messiah, the Christ, a small voice inside him said, *But you don't really believe that either!*

Haslam said later that he could not recall everything he went on to say that day but he remembered a wonderful light and joy filling his soul. Then a local Methodist preacher in the congregation jumped up and shouted, 'The parson is converted! The parson is converted! Hallelujah!' This was followed by at least 20 people calling out for God to save them.[41]

---

[41] Haslam wrote about these events in his memoir, *From Death Into Life*, and elsewhere. Some think that the local Methodist preacher who called out was Billy Bray but he met Haslam sometime later. In his biography of Bray, *The King's Son*, F W Bourne tells how, many years before, when only a few people lived in the area and no church was planned, Bray felt

From then onwards, Haslam preached Christ Jesus the Lord, as the Saviour to sinners. He no longer preached doctrines to be believed and sacraments to be observed, in the hope of getting salvation at some future time! But, as he was careful to point out, he did not neglect either the doctrines or the sacraments. 'Far from it!' he wrote. From then onwards, he explained, they were placed in their proper position: doctrines to saved sinners, as means through which their spiritual life was to be nourished; sacraments, blessed channels through which grateful adoring love might flow up towards God, in obedience to his will.

Revival continued while Haslam was in Cornwall and then seemed to follow him all his life. He ministered in Bristol, Norfolk and London. He was influential in the lives of the people who began the Keswick Conventions and preached at some early ones. When he was in his 80s, although he was by then blind, he conducted Keswick-style conventions around India. He eventually moved to England's south coast, where he preached in the local pavilion on Sunday afternoons and produced a magazine called, *Praise*. He died there in January 1905.

Although this story does not touch on the main theme of this book, I mention William Haslam, not simply from a sense of nostalgia but for two practical reasons. First, because it was an early lesson to me that revival can come within any church tradition. Until then, I had the idea that it happened only among evangelical churches. Second, because Haslam needed to see the futility of promoting spiritual lifestyle without spiritual life. Deriving principles for obtaining and using money from the Bible can contribute towards the highest goals of personal financial education, equipping and empowering people to

---

compelled to pray for revival there.

make their own good choices, but far more important is introducing them to a living relationship with God.

The Primacy of Love

Although the Protestant Reformation of the 16th Century is seen by many as a revival, because it restored emphasis to neglected doctrines, the behaviour of some of the leaders who differed theologically was often rude and offensive, falling far short of the fellowship that is usual among Christians experiencing revival. But in the 1720s, when Protestant Christian refugees from Moravia began to arrive at the estate of Count Zinzendorf in Saxony, they were ashamed of their divisions and recognised that they did not please God. They committed themselves to close fellowship, to worship and pray together, and to care for each other. This was the Moravian Revival of 1727, which was the second revival to inspire me as a young Christian.

Something that impressed me greatly about the Moravians was how their theological discussions did not continue for long without everyone pausing to think about how Jesus had died on a cross for them all. This reflection, they found, brought Jesus into the centre of their experience and put all their theological differences into perspective. Their times for prayer and fellowship increased and a new desire to better understand the Bible gripped them. Then, on Wednesday 13 August 1727, as they prepared for Holy Communion, a new sense of fellowship engulfed them and many remaining differences became less important. At the service, they experienced the presence of God, a nearness of Jesus Christ, as none of them had ever known before. They later spoke of it as their Pentecost. It was the first stirrings of a revival that became known as the Great Awakening that engulfed America and Europe.

What happened should not surprise us. When Jesus first mentioned the church to his disciples, he said that it would have 'the keys of the kingdom of heaven' and that 'the gates of hell shall not prevail against it' (Matthew 16:17-19). Later, he spelled out in more detail the responsibility he was entrusting to it in what we now call The Great Commission, where we learn that all authority in heaven and on earth has been given to Jesus and that his followers are to be 'clothed' with the power of the Holy Spirit in order to make disciples of all nations.[42]

But throughout my lifetime, the church – at least, the church in 'Western' society – has failed to prevail against the gates of consumerism, much less crash the gates of hell. I think the explanation of this failure is found in something Jesus told his disciples in the hours before his arrest. It is preserved for us in John 13:34-35.

> *A new commandment I give to you, that you love one another: just as I have loved you, you also are to love one another. By this all people will know that you are my disciples, if you have love for one another.*

Jesus identified the one thing that would distinguish people who called themselves Christian as truly his disciples, the one criterion by which everyone else could judge their authenticity. Their love for each other.

Claims of religious allegiance, spiritual devotion and even right theology are inadequate to distinguish true Christians from the rest of society. Only Christian love will do that! I am sure this is why the lack of love among the Christians at Corinth was so important to Paul.

In his first letter, Paul criticised the way they met together with bread and wine to remember Jesus. Those who arrived first ate and drank all they wanted, partying well and even getting drunk, leaving nothing for those who arrived later. I expect this reflected the social divide:

---

[42] See Matthew 28:18-20, Mark 16:15-18, Luke 24:46-49 & John 20:21-23.

the richer Christians could arrive earlier than those who had to work long hours, like servants and slaves. People must have seen that going on and asked each other, quite rightly, *What's so different about these Christians?*

Paul also criticised the way the Christian businessmen took each other to court, not to resolve genuine disputes in areas of legitimate difference of opinion, but to expose each other's cheating! People would have seen that going on and asked themselves, quite rightly, *What's so different about these Christians?*

Paul wanted the Christians to love each other. He sought to inspire them with his brilliant description of the nature and effect of love in the passage we now know as 1 Corinthians 13. The passage comes in the middle of his discussion about spiritual gifts, which I assume had become disproportionately important to the Christians.

After explaining that even if he had the ability to speak in many languages, even the languages of angels, and if he had prophetic powers that enabled him to understand all mysteries and all knowledge, and if he had sufficient faith to order mountains to move and to offer himself for martyrdom, it would not amount to much if he did not also love. Without love, it would all be just so much noise – amounting to nothing and gaining him nothing! He then explained what love is, not with a dictionary definition but by illustration.

> *Love is patient and kind; love does not envy or boast; it is not arrogant or rude. It does not insist on its own way; it is not irritable or resentful; it does not rejoice at wrongdoing, but rejoices with the truth. Love bears all things, believes all things, hopes all things, endures all things. Love never ends.*

It is neither our theology nor our good works that mark us as genuine disciples of Jesus. It is our love for each other, expressed in the ways that Paul describes. We may be, of course, truly Christian without that love but we cannot expect other people to see that. Perhaps the most they will see is that we are religious! I am sure this is why the Gospel, which by definition is good news – because that is what the word 'Gospel' means – is generally perceived as bad news! It is why Christians are seen as introspective, legalistic, mechanistic, critical, bigoted and worse! It is not that we can take lightly our own spirituality. We should maintain certain standards of behaviour and practise our devotions by ourselves and in meetings; we should be concerned with helping people in need and addressing the trends in society that create need. But all that counts for little if we do not practise the quality of love that Paul describes!

In church history there are, tragically, many, many examples of Christians falling out viciously over the most trivial points of doctrine. They denounce each other as heretics and apostates. Sometimes these are no more than matters of emphasis or the use of terminology! These controversies are often brought to public attention in the hope of demonstrating who really has 'truth' but I doubt this approach has ever led to revival.

Sometimes the rivalry is less obvious. Many years ago, I was asked by a church to research and implement a project to help people in debt. I discovered that a neighbouring church already had such a project and suggested that the two churches cooperate. But it soon became clear – although it was said explicitly only in jest – that the other church was seen as a rival and that this rivalry was the motivation behind the new initiative: what one could do, the other needed to do better!

John wrote a lot about love. In his first letter, he defined God's essential character as 'God is love' and when he defined love itself he did not use adjectives but example. 'By this we know love' he wrote, 'that [Jesus] laid down his life for us'. He then appends this challenge,

'And we ought to lay down our lives for the brothers'. When such love is visible in churches, the good news about Jesus will be clear and convincing and fewer people would be able to ignore it.

The Way of Fidelity

As I have read about some of the great Christian revivals, I have been struck by the desire of many writers to try to document their origins and progress. This became particularly clear to me as I read about the Welsh Revival. Some think it began at the Welsh Keswick Convention, held in August 1904. Others believe it began the following month, at a church in another part of Wales, when the minister asked a young people's meeting, 'What does Jesus mean to you?' The question seemed to embarrass the group because they were committed Christians and their entire social life revolved around the church. Eventually, one of them said, 'Jesus is the light of the world'. The minister agreed but repeated his question with added emphasis on the pronoun: 'What does Jesus mean to ***you***.' Then a young woman who had been a committed Christian only a week said, 'I love Jesus with all my heart'. Her authenticity transformed the meeting and inspired the minister to arrange for the young people to help him in a series of evangelistic meetings.

Not long after that, one of the leading evangelists in Wales visited that church and experienced a move of God unlike anything he had known previously. He then spoke about what had happened at the theological college where a former coal miner, Evan Roberts, was studying. As a result, the students were given time to attend the evangelist's next series of meetings. It was at one of those meetings, in October, that some believe the Revival began, when Evan Roberts, following the evangelist's example, prayed as an act of consecration, 'Lord, bend me'.

Evan Roberts had already been praying for revival for 11 years. Now that it looked like it would finally come, he withdrew his life savings to pay for himself and a small team to travel around holding evangelistic meetings. He said that he was prepared to pay God for the privilege of preaching. But in the event, he felt called by God to first return home to talk to the young people at his local church in Loughor.

At first, the minister was reluctant to allow the young student to speak at a regular meeting. But after an evening meeting on 4 November, the minster invited the congregation to stay behind to hear what Roberts had to say. About 17 people stayed and what happened there has also come to be seen as the start of the Revival. Roberts told them that he had a message for them from God and then set out what were to become known as the four principals of the Welsh Revival.

- Confess to God any sin known not previously confessed and put right any wrong done to others.
- Do away with any doubtful habit in our lives.
- Promptly obey the influences of the Holy Spirit in our hearts.
- Openly and publicly confess the Lord Jesus Christ.

The impact of Evan's message was so profound that the people returned each night to pray. About a week later, after spending most of the night praying together, they were woken up by people going to the church, even though no meeting had been scheduled. Some say that this was the start of the Revival.

So, just when did the Welsh Revival start? At the convention in August, at Loughor in November or at some point in between? As remarkable and significant as all these events were, it seems to me that none of them can be said to be the *start* of the Revival. Some Christians would, I know, be quick to say that revival starts in heaven. That is certainly true! But Christians have to respond to the heavenly incentive and I think that each of those responses was as a stepping stone along the way.

I began reading about the East African Revival a few years ago and was fascinated by Joe Church's account in, *Quest for the Highest*. Many parts of the book read like a boy's own adventure, full of courageous deeds of daring-do, but two things impressed me: the incredible hardship the missionaries endured from disease, injury and wild animals; and that revival cannot start anywhere but close to home.

When Dr Church arrived in Africa, he discovered congregations growing in numbers, because there were social advantages to being known as a Christian, but little evidence of faith. There was conflict between missionaries with conservative and liberal theologies and a lack of unity among the three branches of their outreach: pastoral, medical and educational. When a new church opened, the missionaries disagreed about whether to have a robed choir: some thought it helpful to orderly worship while others thought it unnecessary ritual. When Dr Church asked a senior doctor whether it was good to allow the church ministers to visit patients in the hospital wards, the reply was a frosty 'no'. And perhaps an indication of how the local people really felt about the missionaries, they stole from the mission to an extent that only became clear when they were touched by the revival and began to return what they had stolen.

In March 1929, Dr Church spoke at a Bible study in Kampala. Among those present was Simeon Nsibambi, a government health officer who was the son of a prosperous African subchief. Three months later, the two men met again on their way to a service at the cathedral and Nsibambi asked if there was anything Dr Church could add to what he had said at the Bible study. Dr

Church records, 'I had been praying for a long time that God would lead me to one really saved African with whom I could have deep fellowship. God was answering that prayer that Sunday morning, when something happened that changed the course of my missionary career.' The two men spent the next two days together in unhurried Bible reading and praying about the fullness of the Spirit.

When Dr Church took charge of a new hospital at Gahini in Rwanda, he and the church minister made a point of praying together about decisions and cooperating as much as possible. (There was no school there at that time.) Soon, they united the separate Sunday services held in the church and the hospital. Personal holiness and proactive witnessing were prioritised. The African employees at the hospital were no longer referred to as 'boys' but 'staff'. And as the Revival gained momentum, Africans and Europeans ministered alongside each other as equals.[43]

The thing that impressed me most about the East African Revival was its ordinariness. There were some noisy, excited meetings but, on the whole, the revival was an extended period in which thousands of people quietly came to faith in Jesus, living in fellowship with him and with each other. More than any other history of revival that I have read, *Quest for the Highest* emphasises how there is nothing irregular, exaggerated or abnormal in revival. On the contrary, it brings normality to a compromised Christianity. I think this was why the Revival continued for over 30 years.

---

[43] This continued in the teams that later took the message of revival to Europe, America and elsewhere. Incidentally, Dr Church wrote up the teaching 'rooted in revival' in his book, *Every Man a Bible Student*, published in 1938 and revised in 1976. In its simplicity, it is lists of Bible references with minimal commentary.

Duncan Campbell is often credited with starting the Hebrides Revival (also called the Lewis Awakening) in 1949. Although he is on record to say that the claim grieved him beyond words, it does seem that when he arrived on the Isle of Lewis the revival spread from the church into the community. When he got off the boat, he went straight to the church. After the service, as the congregation was leaving, they discovered a large crowd of people outside. Campbell preached again and the meeting continued until the morning. Later, they learned that, at the same time, another crowd had gathered spontaneously outside the local police officer's home because he was known to be a Christian.

Campbell's view was that the Revival started a long time before he arrived, when two elderly sisters began to pray through the night for revival. Their particular concern was that none of the young people on the island attended a church. One night, one of the sisters had a vision of the local church crowded with young people and a minister she did not recognise standing in the pulpit.[44] She shared this vision with the minister, who was so gripped by what he heard that he called the church leadership together to pray on Tuesday and Friday nights.

At one of these special prayer meetings about six weeks later, someone read from Psalm 24. 'I will pour water on him that is thirsty, floods upon the dry ground'. Then a young man read from the same Psalm, 'Who shall ascend the hill of God? Who shall stand in His holy place? He that has clean hands and a pure heart who has not lifted up his soul unto vanity or sworn deceitfully. He shall receive the blessing of the Lord'. And then that young man turned to the others present with the words I have already quoted.

[44] She later recognised Duncan Campbell as the preacher in her vision.

It seems to me to be so much humbug to be praying as we are praying, to be waiting as we are waiting, if we ourselves are not rightly related to God.

Duncan Campbell explained what happened next.

And then he lifted his two hands – I'm telling you just as the minister told me it happened – he lifted his two hands and prayed, 'God, are my hands clean? Is my heart pure?' But he got no further. That young man fell to his knees and then fell into a trance.

The start of each of these revivals I have described, and of every other revival I have researched, is impossible to determine, as each was the culmination of people's on-going faithfulness to what they believed God was doing and wanted to do next. And the way of fidelity continued. This was particularly marked in Wales where drunkenness reduced and, as a result, pubs closed. Fewer children were born outside marriage. Debts were repaid, even debts that were so old they could no longer be enforced through the courts.

The Holy Spirit in Revival

When Jesus described how the Holy Spirit works, he likened it to wind that, 'blows where it wishes'. He added, 'You hear its sound, but you do not know where it comes from or where it goes…' While meteorology may now be able to pinpoint the origin of wind, that was not possible when Jesus spoke and it is not possible for most of us. We feel the wind and can see where it has been by what it has done but we cannot calculate its origin or forecast its final destination. So it is with the Holy Spirit, who is not a force of nature but a divine person.

Like almost everything God does, he wants his people involved. 'The Holy Ghost works in us and upon us', John Owen wrote in the 17th Century', but then added an important clarification – '*as we are fit to be wrought in and upon*'. That means, as we a capable of allowing the Holy Spirit to work within us.

Imagine that you have a variety of bottles of different shapes and sizes. You can fill each one to the brim but they will not all hold the same amount of liquid. It is the same with us. The Holy Spirit will only fill us as we are capable of being filled. This is what Owen wrote.

> *The Holy Ghost works in us and upon us, as we are fit to be wrought in and upon; that is, so as to preserve our own liberty and free obedience. He works upon our understandings, wills, consciences, and affections, agreeably to their own natures; he works in us and with us, not against us or without us; so that his assistance is an encouragement as to the facilitating of the work, and no occasion of neglect as to the work itself.*

It is the same with us, although (unlike lifeless bottles) we have the ability and responsibility to increase our own capacity. This is more than being roused by energetic worship, captivated by great preaching or awed by beautiful liturgy. It is, usually, a quiet, enduring work deep in our souls to which we must give priority.

A work of God, as we might call some extraordinary event or movement, is often in response to a stirring in the hearts of one or more Christians. While God was the inspiration and instigator of that stirring, nonetheless, the people involved needed to respond. Writing in Ephesians 4, Paul warned the Christians about grieving the Holy Spirit in their personal lives; in 1 Thessalonians 5, he warned the church against quenching the Holy Spirit. These are warnings we must take seriously if we wish to see revival.

I have heard a few preachers say that God never sends fire on an empty altar. They were thinking of fire as a symbol of the Holy Spirit, and of the times in Israel's history when fire fell from heaven to supernaturally ignite animal sacrifices, and of Paul's use of this imagery in his letter to the Christians in Rome. He wrote, 'present your bodies as a living sacrifice, holy and acceptable to God, which is your spiritual worship'.[45]

I have heard other preachers say that God will not fill dirty vessels. Writing to Timothy, Paul likened Christians to vessels in a great house: some of gold and silver, others made of wood and clay; some for honourable purposes, some for dishonourable.[46] 'Therefore' he wrote, 'if anyone cleanses himself from what is dishonourable, he will be a vessel for honourable use, set apart as holy, useful to the master of the house, ready for every good work.' Whatever type of 'vessel' we may think represents us, our need is to be clean. Paul therefore offered this advice.

> *So flee youthful passions and pursue righteousness, faith, love, and peace, along with those who call on the Lord from a pure heart. Have nothing to do with foolish, ignorant controversies; you know that they breed quarrels…*

Duncan Campbell wrote, 'God will not pour His Holy Spirit into that which is polluted by failure. God wants a clean vessel. Are we clean?' He continued.

> *I think again of those people in the Hebrides. How they longed and how they prayed and how they waited and how they cried, 'Oh God, rend the heavens and come down', and all the time God was handling them; all the time God was dealing with them and the process of cleansing went on until the moment came when angels and archangels looking over the battlements of glory, cried, 'God, the*

---

[45] See Matthew 3:11, Luke 3:16, Acts 2:1-4, Romans 12:1-2, 2 Chronicles 7:1 & 1 Kings 18:38.

[46] See 2 Timothy 2:19-26.

vessels are clean, the miracle can happen now'.

Dr Church had a very simple way of explaining how revival begins. It is when a Christian allows the Holy Spirit 'to take you by your hand' and lead you up Calvary hill to kneel at the foot of the cross. The Holy Spirit has only one vital work, said Church, which is to take us to Jesus. At the cross, the Holy Spirit puts his hand on the back of your head, gently bends your stiff neck and tells you in a still small voice to wait there. When you open your eyes, you see the blood coming down fresh from the wounds of Jesus. Fresh blood, quite fresh, because it is there all the time waiting for sin. And the Holy Spirit brings to your mind any sin that you know is there.

When the Holy Spirit shows you what things need to be put right with your neighbour, he says clearly to you, hold out your heart, hold out your cup and the water of life will flow in and fill it. He will fill it when there is nothing left at the bottom to be cleansed away, because Jesus on the cross has already drunk the dregs of the shame and the cost of your sin. You must put right any feelings about others, Dr Church explained, feelings about anyone whom you would not want to meet. The Spirit will tell you to put out your hand and to take that person's hand in reconciliation and fellowship.

It is as two Christians link at the foot of Jesus' cross, forming 'the smallest revival team', that revival begins. 'It is not with great preaching', Church told a conference in England, 'not with mass meetings but on and on, two by two, one getting another, two making four, four making eight.'

He used an illustration, a parable, that I found very helpful. One day a man arrived at the hospital in Gahini and, as soon as Dr Church saw the man, he saw a patch of leprosy on the man's forehead. Church got a small mirror and showed the patch to the man. 'That's alright', the man said, 'I've come for medicine for my inside.' Dr Church's

African aide had to then explain to the man that he had the dreaded disease of leprosy, even though he was unable to see it for himself.

In the same way, we are often unaware of the sin we pick up from those around us and it is as if the Holy Spirit has to hold up a mirror for us to see it. And perhaps, for another Christian to explain its implications. That is why transparency in fellowship is important to revival. We do not have to confess publicly every sin, as many sins committed privately can be confessed and repented of privately without maintaining a pretence of virtue. But, whether repentance is private or public, restitution should be made where possible.

A Personal Conviction

Revival comes not when our emotions are riding high and our worship is about to raise the roof but when we quietly and thoughtfully get real with God and right with each other. While attitudes to money, the ways we get it and use it, are not the only lifestyle choices that we need to bring into line with Jesus' teaching, unless we do include money, our best intentions are incomplete and inadequate in a consumer society.

Jesus gave a high priority to his followers using money in ways that showed that they did not serve money. *Arguably, a higher priority than to sexual purity.* He warned us to avoid all covetousness. And of the religious elite who taught that God rewards the righteous with material wealth, he said they exalted what is an abomination in the sight of God.

The greatest hindrances to prayer for revival are unclean hands and impure hearts. I urge you to return to the earlier chapters in this book and ask yourself again some of the questions I pose about the ways you think about money and handle it. Your attitude may be less selfish and extravagant than may seem to be the accepted norm today, and you may live more modestly than your neighbours and work colleagues, but money may nonetheless be for you an 'Asherah pole' alongside your trust in God.

Some pastors warn against debt and describe the obligations it creates as a form of bondage, which is certainly true. Some may go as far as criticising purchases that undermine the ability to live responsible, healthy lives, such as unnecessarily expensive houses and cars that are expensive to run with high credit repayments. Some may even prioritise tithing above these sorts of indulgences. But rarely, it seems to me, are congregations challenged to address their basic attitude to money, their disposition towards it.

To grasp what Jesus said, we need to see his point without formulating it into a list of dos and don'ts which could so very easily lead us into tick-box legalism. Jesus told his disciples to do a difficult thing – a very difficult thing! – to use mammon, the power of money, without serving mammon. To use it wisely, to use it to make friends without being influenced by its power or letting it compromise in any way our service to God. That is not just very hard to do but it is hard to describe and why I included Dr Church's description of how revival begins.

All power has the potential to corrupt people and it is not limited to the very powerful. We have all, I expect, heard how power can corrupt politicians, government officials and church pastors as well as rich people. It can corrupt people with just a little power, like frontline officials and clerks, as readily as people at the top. A sure sign that power is corrupting is the corrosion of accountability. Powerful people often think they are above the law, above even the norms of civilised society. They lie and insult people; they make selfish decisions arbitrarily with impunity. And very often, they get away with it just because we have even come to expect it of powerful people.

Mammon has the power to corrupt everyone, rich and poor. It corrupts those who have money and those who want it, those who want to accumulate it for its own sake and those who want the indulgences and status symbols it can buy them. Whether we hope to get away with pilfering office stationery or embezzling a million pounds, the power corrupts. And it corrupts God's people in ways so subtle that we do not realise what is happening, because it all seems so very normal in the world.

A sure sign of the astonishing power of mammon is that many Christians seem to think that the Bible has nothing to say on the ways we earn and use money or that it is something preachers ought to comment on. I first began to think about this more than 20 years ago, after hearing a sermon by Ray Steadman. He was minister of Peninsula Bible Church in California for 40 years from 1950 and the sermon, preached in 1964, is called, *God or Mammon.*[47] 'Traditionally, this is a very sensitive subject', he begins. 'When the subject of a message is the matter of money or possessions, preachers are frequently accused of losing their spirituality and beginning to meddle in affairs that do not concern them.'

I have often found that to be the case and have even been accused of perverting the Gospel message by saying that Jesus taught about money. Pastor Stedman's clarification is not unique to him but I quote it because I think it is now less well understood by Christians than it was during 'the swinging 60s'.

> *I find that objection arises from a distorted concept of Christian living – the idea that is so frequently*

---

[47] I downloaded the transcript of the sermon from raystedman.org on 4 December 2019 and it is from that transcript that I quote. I have added the emphasis.

> *expressed that 'Religion is one thing, and politics and business quite another'. If that were true I would be the first to suggest that we tear up our Bibles and forget the whole business, because, as James puts it, 'Faith without works is dead', (James 2:20 KJV).* ***That is, faith that does not control your pocketbook (or perhaps, to be more up-to-date, your credit card) is entirely worthless.***

We cannot discern the extent to which we have, ourselves, been infected by avarice. We need to go to the foot of the cross, as Dr Church describes, and let the Holy Spirit gently bend our stiff necks; we need to let the Spirit hold up a mirror to our lives so we can see how we are trying to serve both God and mammon. And we may need someone to help us understand, just as Dr Church's aide had to help the infected man understand his leprosy. That is why Christians need to be real not only with God but with each other, not necessarily revealing every private sin but neither allowing ourselves to be shrouded in an illusion of piety.

A Personal Experience

Many years ago, an event at evangelistic campaign convinced me of how important repentance is to revival. The visiting evangelist used the first meeting to call the church to repentance. He spoke from 2 Chronicles 7:13-14, a passage that tells the Israelites that if they experienced drought, locusts and sickness it will be a consequence of them turning away from God. This is the remedy.

> *If my people who are called by my name humble themselves, and pray and seek my face and turn from their wicked ways, then I will hear from heaven and will forgive their sin and heal their land.*

The evangelist explained that we can think of drought,

locusts and sickness in both spiritual and material ways. Is there a drought of people attending churches and coming to faith in the Lord Jesus Christ? Do the children who grew up attending with their parents tend to disappear, as if devoured by locusts? If God were to revive the church, the evangelist said, he would be reviving carnality! Revival must begin in the church for God to bring in new people, he said. The sermon was well-reasoned, relevant and passionate. At the end, the evangelist said he would leave the platform to allow the congregation to pray together and deal with anything amiss in their relations with God or each other.

I closed my eyes as one of the church leaders began to pray. He did not confess any 'terrible' sin such as dishonesty or immorality but such sins as a lack of love to God and neglecting private devotional time; a lack of concern for fellow Christians and a preoccupation with material things. He prayed for about four or five minutes. When he finished, I waited for someone else to pray but nobody did. When I opened my eyes, I saw that there were only three of us still in the congregation. In those few minutes, about 50 people had quietly slipped out of the building. I looked behind me and saw two other church leaders standing by the door waiting to lock up.

I had been completely unaware that the people were leaving. I was astounded that so many people could move so quickly and quietly!

The only time I heard that event mentioned was a week later, on the last day of the campaign, when I happened to overhear one church leader say to another that there had been no need for the man to pray as he did. By that time, it seemed that throughout all of the evangelistic services, coffee mornings, children's meetings and open air witnessing, nobody had come to believe on Jesus. But as I was writing this chapter, I was reminiscing with a friend and he told me that he knew of one, someone who had attended church all her life but had never before made a personal commitment to Jesus.

My friend also told me that he remembered the evangelist saying on another evening that if the church did not repent, God would close it within a year. In the event, the church did not close until a few months ago. But in the intervening years, it seemed to survive only because people moved to it having split from their previous churches over some issue. A few years ago it stopped holding Sunday evening services because it could not find people willing to preach. Today, the building is being used by another church fellowship. When my friend and I discussed this, and wondered if it was the fulfilment of what the evangelist had warned, we remembered how King Saul continued to reign for 20 years after God 'tore' the Kingdom from him.[48]

There is a time and place for loud, enthusiastic worship in services. Christians have always sung psalms, hymns and songs that celebrate the majesty of God, his unfailing love for us and our eternal security as Christians. And we have always praised God's unstoppable mission to establish his Kingdom here on earth. But when our worship is triumphant, when we confidently affirm God's love for us in all circumstances and energetically declare our faith in what he wants to do in our generation, we should remember that this is not how God said we should pray for revival. We are to humble ourselves to pray, to turn from our wicked ways as we seek God's face, for only then will he hear from heaven and will forgive our sin and heal our land.

A Necessary Emphasis

Vance Havner (1901-1986) preached repentance across America for over 70 years. He grew up in the hills of

---

[48] See 1 Samuel 15.

North Carolina and, in his own words, 'lived the simple, happy life of an old-fashioned country boy'. He preached with a distinctive southern accent that enhanced his humour but his messages were serious and uncompromising. He taught that a Christian should exhibit faithfulness to Jesus in all areas of life.

He told the story of a group of young boys who went off to a field to play football. When they arrived, they realised none of them had the ball. After they argued about it for a while, one of them said, 'Never mind the ball, let's get on with the game!' Havner used that unforgettable story to describe the folly of expecting revival without repentance.

The Bible contains the testimony of a wise man of God who was corrupted by great wealth. King Solomon was so wise and so rich that he was able to exhaust the potential of money. He was wise because God gave him special wisdom. When he became Israel's king, Solomon built the first temple in Jerusalem. Soon after that, God appeared to him in a dream and said, 'Ask what I shall give you'. God offered Solomon a blank cheque and to his eternal credit he did not ask for wealth, a long life or victory in war but for wisdom. This pleased God, who gave Solomon not only wisdom but additionally riches and honour – so much so that 'no other king shall compare with you all your days'.

King Solomon ranks among the very wealthiest people in all history. There may be people today with greater wealth than Solomon but it is stored as credit data in computer systems and cannot be converted into the volume of material goods that Solomon owned. Solomon could see and touch his great wealth! He understood the value of money and there are many references to it in his contributions to the book of Proverbs in the Hebrew Scriptures.[49]

We read there that a rich man's wealth is his strong city but the poverty of the poor is their ruin; that wealth brings many new friends but a poor man is deserted by his friend. Solomon warned against accumulating wealth dishonestly and reckoned some things more important than wealth. Better is a little with the fear of the Lord than great treasure and trouble with it, he wrote; better a little with righteousness than great revenues with injustice; better a poor person who walks in his integrity than one who is crooked in speech and a fool.

But the way that Solomon accumulated unparalleled wealth, particularly through the trading expeditions he sponsored, betrayed his growing avarice. In Deuteronomy 17, the part of God's law governing Israelite kings, they are forbidden from accumulating horses and, specifically, from getting them from Egypt, the world leader in horse breeding. The law continues, 'And [a king] shall not acquire many wives for himself, lest his heart turn away, nor shall he acquire for himself excessive silver and gold'. But all this is just what Solomon did!

Solomon not only brought horses from Egypt but also married Pharaoh's daughter, possibly for no better reason

[49] The book of Proverbs is a compilation that has been through the hands of many editors during the past 3,000 years. There is good reason to believe that the first nine chapters were in fact the last of Solomon's writing to be included and that the section beginning at Chapter 25, compiled by King Hezekiah's court, may have been the earliest. The last two chapters in the book are introduced as being the accumulated wisdom of other people, including Agur who I mentioned earlier. In the paragraph that follows, I have not given references as they are samples intended only to give a flavour of the character and wisdom of their author. I recommend reading the entire collection and collating for yourself everything relevant to money, wealth, debt and poverty.

than to cement a trade deal. Solomon married many other foreign women and began to adopt their pagan gods. He not only allowed Asherah poles in the fields but also a temple to the goddess. Gradually, his life became an abomination before God. Although he repented and recovered from this apostasy, he stands an example of how wealth can create greater temptations than poverty.

- Do you believe that God has blessed you with natural skills and spiritual gifts that you use in his service? Solomon was blessed like that.
- Have you experienced God's blessing on your ministry? Solomon's people enjoyed unprecedented prosperity during his reign.
- Have you founded ministries and churches? Solomon built a magnificent temple in Jerusalem.
- Have you witnessed incredible answers to prayer and signs and wonders? At the dedication of the new temple, the cloud of God's glory filled it so mightily that the priests could not stand to minister! After Solomon prayed, supernatural fire ignited the sacrifices and, again, God's glory filled the temple!
- Is your life full of good things, desirable 'fruit and flowers': a taste for fine food and wine, for example, or an appreciation of the latest fashion and tech? So was Solomon's life while he gradually became an abomination to God without realising it!

After Vance Havner preached about repentance at a church service in a small town, one of the leaders thought Havner had been too hard on the congregation. He explained, 'Well, we're not so good in this town, but we're not so bad either. We try to make an honest living, pay our debts and behave ourselves. We're not so good but we're not so bad.' Havner replied, 'But don't you remember, that is the kind of people who made the Lord sick?'

Havner was referring to the Christians at Laodicea, who thought they were rich but who Jesus said were destitute. On the basis of what Jesus told them, recorded in Revelation 3:14-22, Havner used to say that the Lord's last word to his people was not the Great Commission, the command to make disciples, but the call to repent.[50]

The Price of Revival

As I explained at the start, a conviction that has been growing in me for more than 20 years is that no church will experience revival unless its people get a right attitude to money. This may not have been an issue for Christians in the past but I am certain that it is now.

I go further! It is almost certainly the case that no church will experience revival unless its ministers and leaders have a right attitude to money. Read the prophet Malachi's book: although the people had sinned, God blamed the priests because it was they who had overlooked the people's behaviour, allowed them to withhold their tithes and accepted their defective sacrifices at the Temple.

We must be careful to remember, however, that revival cannot itself become the centre of our desire. Only Jesus himself can be that. And not only must he be central, there must not be anything else close enough to distract us from him. Even a right concern for Jesus' reputation and testimony in the world, and a desire to introduce people to Jesus by evangelism and revival, should not detract from Jesus himself.

Some time ago, I was reminded of Leonard Ravenhill's observation made in (I think) 1970 or 1971.

---

[50] I have written more about Laodicea in the fourth appendix, *A Church in Need of Renewal.*

'I offer it as my considered judgment that the main reason why we do not have heaven-born, Spirit-operated revival in our day is that we are content to live without it.' He added, 'Lesser "blessings" make us happy. Another bus for Sunday School is all that some ask. A bigger attendance this year at Easter and Christmas elevates the joy of many promotion-geared churches. Others boast in a bigger offering for missions.'

This reminded me of something Evan Roberts said to J Edwin Orr in about 1935.[51]

> *People ask me, my brother, if I see any signs of the revival [for which] we all pray. Now, as you travel about, you may see the positive signs, but I am not so privileged just now. I tell them that I see all the negative signs. The churches seem to be at rock-bottom in their decline. The turning point is at hand.*
>
> *Indeed, I would compare the state of the true church today with the state of the prodigal son in the far country just before he went home to his father. Mark you, he has not started for home yet...he is still among the swine and the husks, but he is 'utterly fed-up'. As I would have said of the prodigal son, 'He won't be there much longer', so I predict of the church as it is today.*

In the light of history, it seems that Evan Roberts' prediction was far too optimistic. While there have been rare exceptions, rather than leave the pig pen, most Christians deal with their dissatisfaction by accommodating themselves to it and finding new ways to make the pigs' husks seem more exciting!

During the years of the Toronto Blessing, I heard many reports of physical healing. I personally experienced

[51] J Edwin Orr reported the conversation in his book, *The Church Must First Repent*, published in 1937.

healing of a minor but longstanding physical problem. But the 'healing' miracles that baffled me began in 1999, when people started reporting that their dental fillings had turned to gold! Without exception, I heard people say how wonderful this was. Some even said that it was harder for God to replace the fillings with gold than to heal the teeth! Another enigma at that time was gold dust appearing from nowhere at meetings. I saw this twice. Once I saw it glittering on the preacher's jacket but I was some way from the platform and could not tell whether it was a genuine miracle or, as I heard some say, a stage trick. But the second time, I was in a small group listening to a Bible study when the speaker suddenly stopped and pointed to the glittering dust sprinkled across her open Bible. I was close enough to believe that it was not a trick. But I found it hard to believe the generally accepted explanation that this was a foretaste of God's coming glory.

Why gold? I puzzled over that for a long while. Why were the people's teeth not healed? After all, imagine the reaction if a person missing a hand, or with a weak heart, were 'healed' by a prosthetic hand or a pacemaker! And why get so very excited about gold dust when we pray for revival? Is it because we are too easily satisfied, happy with a little glitter in the pig pen?

The price of revival in a consumer society is money itself. Or, rather, mammon: the power of money. Unless we forsake it, we will be forever trying to serve God and mammon. Although material wealth does not hinder every Christian, none of us living in a consumer society can risk complacency. But if we think these things off limits, nobody else's business and outside the remit of pastors and prophets, it is a certain proof that we have been corrupted by mammon.

Our repentance before God must include more than our attitude to money but, unless it does include money, it is incomplete and inadequate. Jesus' paradigm for handling money should help us identify our weaknesses and failings.

I pray this book will be a catalyst, helping God's people to root out the love of money from their thoughts and their theology. I pray that it may be used by the Holy Spirit to help them to recognise avarice, coveting, greed and other financial sins and lead them to repentance – to discipleship, contentment and generosity. And I pray that it may promote revival in churches that will lead to spiritual awakening in the wider communities they serve. I close with this quote from Duncan Campbell.

> *It is one thing to shout it, it is one thing to sing it, it is one thing to talk about revival, but give me a people on their faces, seeking to be rightly related with God, and when that happens, we will soon know the impact of God-realisation in our country.*

POSTSCRIPT: THE BOTTOM LINE

Theoretically, philosophically, I may be quite willing to accept that there is a higher reality... But when it comes to money – ah, that is usually quite a different matter... Everywhere [money] is still understood, often even more forcibly than in matters of illness and death, as representing the 'real world' – the 'bottom line'.

Professor Jacob Needleman,
Money and the Meaning of Life

Among the visual aids I use in my talks is a million dollar banknote. As it is so valuable, no American President is worthy of having his picture on it and there is a picture of the Statue of Liberty instead! Of course, nobody is taken in by it. At least, nobody in any of my audiences. It is clearly a novelty banknote. And yet, I have read news stories of people trying to use one. I have heard of a couple of people who tried to deposit them at banks. When a man tried to use one at his local supermarket, the sales assistant called the manager only because she did not have enough cash to give the man change!

I also have some 'real' money that sounds more impressive than it is. I have a bank note with a face value of fifty million dollars issued in Zimbabwe in 2008 but I doubt that it would have bought a single loaf of bread. I have two coins, made of very cheap metal, that each has a face value of half a million marks. They were circulating in Germany after World War 1 but their novelty value today is greater than anything they could buy then.

My point is, you can trust money only when everyone else trusts it. By contrast, we can always trust Jesus Christ, which is why I want to close by explaining more about his authority to teach. The 'bottom line' is the final line on a financial report that shows the net profit or loss, which is often all that matters to a business or person hoping to do well. Metaphorically, it refers to the key fact in a situation or the final result of an activity. In my view, Jesus of Nazareth is the ultimate 'bottom line'.

When the Temple intellectuals wondered how Jesus, a carpenter from Galilee with no more than an elementary education, spoke like one of them, he told them. The incident is recorded in John 6. 'My teaching is not mine, but his who sent me', he explained. This accounts for the overview effect of his teaching: his ability to see life from a distance. But while many people have claimed similar authority, Jesus then added something astonishing. 'If anyone's will is to do God's will, he will know whether the teaching is from God or whether I am speaking on my own authority.' But as outrageous as that sounds, the whole of John's Gospel was written to explain that Jesus spoke and acted with God's authority because he *is* God.[52]

> *Now Jesus did many other signs in the presence of the disciples, which are not written in this book;* ***but these are written*** *so that you may believe that Jesus is the Christ, the Son of God, and that by believing you may have life in his name.*

Jesus of Nazareth was not like the Roman emperors, who claimed to be gods but still died like men. Had he been no more than they, belief in him would have died out within a few generations and I would not have even thought about writing this book. But Jesus consistently declared

[52] John 20:30-31.

that he stood before men and women in the place of God: that when they heard his words, they had heard God; when they saw his works, they had seen God at work. And, ultimately, if any believed on him they were believing on God.

Jesus must have been either deranged or genuine. To look on him as simply, 'a good man', is not rational: nobody who is good says those sorts of things! I realise that, rather than simply dismiss Jesus as delusional, many people try to come to terms with his claim by saying that it was attributed to him posthumously. But, it seems to me, his claims are so closely woven into everything the Gospels tell us about him, that to reject them leaves us with nothing remarkable or worthy of our attention.

I am therefore driven to the conclusion that Jesus of Nazareth is Almighty God, God the Son who 'has come in the flesh'. He did not come on a simple rescue mission, to save individual people from hell. Although he did do this, he had a much grander, more comprehensive purpose: to reconcile together into one all things in heaven and earth and then to present them to the Father. To this end, he died on a cross.

Three days later, his Father, God the Father, raised Jesus from the dead and 'seated him at his right hand in the heavenly places, far above all rule and authority and power and dominion, and above every name that is named, not only in this age but also in the one to come. And he put all things under his feet and gave him as head over all things…'[53]

It is on this authority that we can and should live as he taught. Although there is more to this than the ways we get and use money, unless these ways do comply with what he taught, then it is certain that we cannot get far with anything else. We see this demonstrated when Jesus

[53] Paul writing at the end of Ephesians 1.

met another person who wanted to know how he could be sure he would have eternal life. This one was a rich young ruler and his meeting with Jesus is recorded in three of the Gospels.[54] This is from Matthew's account.

> *And behold, a man came up to him, saying, 'Teacher, what good deed must I do to have eternal life?' And he said to him, 'Why do you ask me about what is good? There is only one who is good. If you would enter life, keep the commandments.' He said to him, 'Which ones?' And Jesus said, 'You shall not murder, You shall not commit adultery, You shall not steal, You shall not bear false witness, Honour your father and mother, and, You shall love your neighbour as yourself.' The young man said to him, 'All these I have kept. What do I still lack? Jesus said to him, 'If you would be perfect, go, sell what you possess and give to the poor, and you will have treasure in heaven; and come, follow me.' When the young man heard this he went away sorrowful, for he had great possessions.*
>
> *And Jesus said to his disciples, 'Truly, I say to you, only with difficulty will a rich person enter the kingdom of heaven. Again I tell you, it is easier for a camel to go through the eye of a needle than for a rich person to enter the kingdom of God.'*

I doubt it was the first time the young man had asked his question about eternal life to a spiritual teacher. At first, Jesus gave what I expect was the same reply the man had

---

[54] See Matthew 19:16-30, Mark 10:17-31 & Luke 18:18-30. The terms eternal life, entering the Kingdom of Heaven, entering the Kingdom of God and being saved refer to the same general experience. Although the Greek words translated eternal life mean, literally, a fullness of life that is perpetual, in John 17:3 eternal life is defined as knowing the only true God and Jesus Christ.

heard many times before: keep the commandments. By that, Jesus meant living the sort of life defined by the Ten Commandments, although it is possible that he added something new when he said, 'You shall love your neighbour as yourself'.

The young man replied that he had done all this since his childhood and Jesus did not seem to doubt it. As a Jew, the man was not claiming any moral or religious perfection, free from all wrongdoing, only that he had lived a sincere and devout life. He was, therefore, like many Christians today. But Jesus then added something radical, 'But you lack one thing', and told the rich young ruler to give away all his wealth to the poor, so that he would have treasure in heaven.

Some have assumed from Jesus' words that the man lacked poverty and conclude that being poor is the preferred situation for all 'true' Christians. But this cannot be right. Not only is there nothing in the Bible to suggest that it is wrong to be wealthy, it mentions wealthy people who were faithful to God. Others believe that Jesus was inviting the man to do more than be a disciple and to join the group that travelled with him. While there is some truth in that, I think it nothing more than a practical consequence of the man giving away his wealth, for the man would then have had no home and been unable to continue functioning as a ruler.

The thing the devout ruler lacked was trust. He believed in and trusted God but it was not unequivocal trust. Jesus challenged him to complete it by transferring to God alone the trust he had in his inherited wealth. The only way for him to do this was by giving away everything.

Why did Jesus omit coveting from the commandments he told the ruler to keep? I think it was because he would soon ask the ruler to go beyond keeping it, to do the very opposite of what it forbade in order to accumulate treasure in heaven. Why did Jesus not tell the ruler about the need to love God with all his heart, soul, mind and strength, as he told the lawyer? I expect because the ruler was not ready to comprehend the enormity of that. But if the ruler had accepted Jesus' invitation to follow, he would have come to know and love both Jesus and his Father.

To continue the story, as the rich young ruler walked away, sorrowful, Jesus told his disciples just how hard it is for a rich person to enter the Kingdom of God: harder than for a camel pass through the eye of a needle! This startled the apostles: 'Who then can be saved?' they asked. I expect they were thinking of themselves because they had not done what Jesus had told the rich young ruler to do.

At least six of the disciples were fishermen. Of these, James and John were the sons of Zebedee, who owned a fishing fleet, while Peter and Andrew were brothers in the family that may have been Zebedee's business partners. Those disciples had left the family businesses but it is likely they could have returned had they wished.[55] Matthew had left his job as a tax collector but he could have got another job. Simon is called a zealot, which suggests he was a politician; if that is correct, it is a strong indication he came from a wealthy family and could have returned to his old way of life.

Jesus had some reassuring words for these men. 'With man this is impossible', he replied, 'but with God all things are possible.' It is important to notice that Jesus did not say that God would do the impossible for rich people, by taking them through the needle's eye. He said that rich people could successfully go through *with* God. That is, with his help.

---

[55] John 21 records what happened when some of the disciples did decide to go fishing again. I mention it because they seem to have had immediate access to a fishing boat.

The subsequent lives of these disciples show that, with the exception of the one who betrayed Jesus, they had all made the commitment that Jesus had asked of the rich young ruler and experienced God's support.

By comparison with most of the people living in the world today, most Christians living in a consumer society are rich! This affluence anchors our perceptions in the physical world and occupies us with secondary things. Not having to worry about where our next meal is coming from, we worry about how it will taste; having many clothes to choose from, we fret about our image; with too much leisure time, we strive for novelty. This addiction to routine comfort can undermine our inner values and higher priorities. While God may not wish us to give away all we own, we should not assume that he is happy for us to continue with 'business as usual'.

Some time ago, I heard about a new Christian during the Jesus Revolution of the 1960s & 70s who withdrew all his savings and, quite literally, threw it away. He actually held the bank notes up to the wind and let them go! But then he realised that he needed money to buy food and to have his shoes repaired. While I commend the young man's clear and uncompromised trust in God, Jesus never said anything to suggest that we should be careless with money. And Paul understood its value to finance ministry and relieve hardship. (But I must add that the Bible says nothing to suggest that either of them could have achieved more with more money!)

I have read biographies of Christians who gave away significant wealth to live in simplicity as pastors and missionaries. And I have read of rich Christians who lived modestly while using their wealth to trade for the good of the community, to provide jobs for people and to fund charitable projects around the world. There is no one right way for all of us but we must all, as a friend once said to me, 'touch the things of this world lightly'. I hope that what I have written about Jesus' paradigm for handling money helps you to see God's way for you.

I remember when I began to see something of who Jesus is. It was in 1968. I did not understand everything that I understand now but I remember lying in bed one night thinking that if Jesus was really who I thought he was, then I ought to get right with him. I knew this required repentance: a complete change of mind and direction for my life. I therefore committed myself to following Jesus, to being his disciple and to living the way he and his immediate followers described.

I am not suggesting that it has been a smooth ride for the past 50 years. In fact, far from it! I have felt very far from God as well as near to him; I have lived up to my commitment inconsistently, often dreadfully and appallingly, but he has been consistently faithful and good. I have, from time to time, been thoroughly confused by what different people said about Jesus and found that the only unerring guide is the Bible itself. But I have never doubted who Jesus is. I still believe: God has kept me.

In the Introduction, I suggested that if you knew more about what Jesus taught, you might want to know more about him as a person. I hope this is true in your case and, if you have not done so already, that you follow up by reading about him in the Gospels. You could begin with Mark's Gospel, which many find the clearest. But although John's Gospel is, in some ways, the hardest to understand, if you focus on the 'signs' that John explains, and seek God's help, you will see that Jesus is the Son of God. And, believing, you can experience eternal life.

Glory to the Father, and to the Son,
and to the Holy Spirit;
As it was in the beginning, is now,
and ever shall be.
Amen.

APPENDIX: FUNDRAISING & GIVING

About 120 years ago, at one of D L Moody's annual conferences held in Massachusetts, the head of an American youth organisation took questions from the audience. 'How shall we raise money for foreign missions?' someone asked. 'Don't raise it', was the immediate reply, 'give it.'

Dr G Campbell Morgan described what happened in a sermon a few years later. He then explained its importance.

> *In that answer is the solution of the whole problem which confronts us at the present hour. If funds are lacking to carry on the work of God in the far distant places of the earth, it is because the church has become so busy raising money that she has ceased to give it.*

Today, there can be no doubt that funds are lacking for churches at home as well as for evangelistic and aid projects abroad. Many churches struggle to pay their bills and believe they have no alternative but to resort to fundraising.

I once heard a preacher say that God never orders a meal that he cannot pay for. I agree. God is well able to cover the cost of everything he wants done. But, as in so many ways, God wants his people to get involved.

- Moses asked the Israelites for their gold and other materials to build the Tabernacle.
- David asked for materials so that his son, Solomon, could build the Temple.

- Paul asked churches for money to relieve a famine in Jerusalem.

God still expects his people to fund his work and, with these examples in mind, no Christian leader should feel ashamed in asking people to fund a project that they believe God has entrusted to them. Simply asking for funding is not fundraising.

Morgan called his sermon, *The Grace of Giving a Million Shillings*, and it was intended to raise awareness of the financial difficulties faced by a British missionary organisation. The need was a consequence of the organisation's success and to curtail the work would, Morgan said, be like cutting down a rose tree on the very day it was about to bloom. Since first reading that sermon, I have often wondered how many projects God has inspired and then allowed to fail for no other reason than the failure of Christians to give.

There is nothing wrong with Christians getting together for social activities, such as quiz nights, and donating any money raised to a good cause. Nor is there anything wrong in Christians setting themselves challenging tasks, such as running a marathon, and asking people to encourage their efforts with donations in support of good causes. And while some Christians are averse to raffles and lotteries for theological or social reasons,[56] others see them as a fun way to involve the wider community in supporting a good cause. But whatever your view of these activities, if they are necessary to motivate Christians to part with their money to keep open their churches and to finance evangelism and poverty relief, then something is very wrong. The money

[56] One theological objection is that the incentive of reward is incompatible with freewill generosity; one social objection is that a lot of research has found that the people most attracted by the hope of winning are the least able to afford to lose.

they pay and gamble could easily have been given out of devotion to God and love for people. The amounts raised would then have been greater because there would have been no administration costs incurred.

When I first began teaching personal finance, a Christian leader told me that Christians would pack seminars about fundraising but rarely turn up to hear about stewardship and giving. I have never tried to teach about fundraising and so have never seen that for myself. But I do know that Christians seem reluctant to hear about stewardship and giving. Yet, when Christians do gather to talk about money, they often want to focus on giving, as if getting that right is the most important thing. But unless all the ways we get and use money conform to Jesus' teaching, our giving will not achieve much.

Supporting churches, missionary and charitable projects is both an obligation and privilege for Christians and, as we should expect, the Bible includes helpful guidance. In the Bible, the number ten is often associated with government and social order, such as the Ten Commandments, and one tenth of our personal prosperity, called a tithe, is our formal, structured contribution towards this.

I have occasionally heard Christians say that they 'tithe' 5% of their income, or some other percentage, but that is a contradiction in terms. The meaning of Hebrew word for tithe is exact: one tenth. But it is equally wrong to make the tithe into a law.

The one tenth principle first appears in the life of Abraham. After rescuing his nephew from an alliance of hostile kings, Abraham visited Melchizedek, God's priest at Salem (later renamed, Jerusalem), and gave him a tithe. It is not clear what Abraham tithed, or whether he ever tithed again. But whatever he did, when his grandson, Jacob, was going into exile, he promised to tithe if God prospered him. Although, again, we do not know how Jacob did this.[57]

The tithe was later enshrined in the Torah, God's 'Law' that governed how the Israelites were to live. It is mentioned in a few places and can be interpreted in various ways but at least two things are clear.

- The Levites, who received the tithe, were themselves to observe the one tenth principle and give a tithe of the tithe to the priests.
- At least some portion of the tithe was for the relief of poverty.[58]

Jesus affirmed the one tenth principle when he criticised some Pharisees for tithing their herbs but disregarding 'weightier matters' of justice, mercy and faithfulness. 'These you ought to have done', he told them, 'without neglecting the others'. While I am sure that Jesus was not saying that we need to be as painstakingly legalistic about tithing as those Pharisees, their giving meant nothing in

[57] For Abraham's tithe, see Genesis 14:17-20. He may have tithed everything he owned, *or* the goods he had accumulated after leaving Babylonia *or* the plunder he took from the defeated kings. For Jacob's tithe, see Genesis 28:20-22. If we think that either man tithed regularly or periodically, we have to ask ourselves how. As there was no Tabernacle or other centre of worship to support, did they go to Melchizedek from time to time? Or give to the poor? I cannot recall hearing any insight about what they might have done to support the claim that they tithed regularly. These doubts, however, do not detract from the significance of what they did and I mention them only to avoid legalism in the application of the principle.

[58] See Leviticus 27:30-33, Numbers 18:21-32 & Deuteronomy 14:22-29. Some scholars think these all refer to a single tithe collected every three years while others understand them as one annual tithe plus a further tithe collected every three years. There are some other interpretations.

light of their disregard of more important responsibilities.[59]

When Paul collected funds from churches to help relieve a famine in Jerusalem, he advised those in Corinth to put aside a proportion of their income each week. While it is not certain that Paul meant to imply one tenth of their income, on balance, I think he probably did. Earlier in the letter, he had explained how Christian ministers should be supported in the same way as those who had served in the Temple: that is, with a tithe.[60]

The one tenth principle is the place to begin thinking about our giving but it is not all that we need to think about. Tithing is a threshold, not a finishing line. It does not exhaust our obligations any more than legalistic Pharisees could ignore justice and mercy. But it is equally important that we remember that tithing is a principle that not all Christians can practise. Those on persistent low incomes are justified in giving less than 10%, because they have a duty before God to look after their families adequately, pay their taxes and repay any debt they owe.[61] They should not feel guilty for not tithing!

But, while I am confident that God is understanding of sincere Christians in difficult circumstances who fail to give 10%, I must now explain another paradox. I have often heard stories of Christians with inadequate income to cover basic needs who nevertheless decided to tithe and gradually discovered that 90% of their income went further than the 100% had done before. The rationale for this can be found in these words of Jesus: 'It is more blessed to give than to receive'.

---

[59] See Matthew 23:23-24 & Luke 11:42.

[60] Consider 1 Corinthians 9:13-14 & 16:1-3.

[61] See, for example, 1 Timothy 5:3-16, Matthew 22:17-21, Romans 13:1-7, Psalm 37:21 & Proverbs 3:27-28.

These words were not reported in any of the Gospels but recorded by Luke in his history of the early church, when Paul quoted them as he said his final goodbye to some church leaders.[62] Although his immediate purpose was to remind them that he had taught for three years without payment, the truth of Jesus' words applies to all Christian giving.[63] But we must remember that this paradox is not an excuse for not repaying debts, paying taxes or looking after dependents properly. In my experience, this not always understood by Christians in debt.

If a creditor will allow you to repay what you owe by instalments, and this allows you to tithe, that is good and you should take the opportunity. But I have often wondered what sort of impression is created by Christians refusing to repay their debts (and sometimes their taxes, also) because of what they see as an obligation to give to their church instead.

Although the one tenth principle is just one important aspect of Christian lifestyle and witness, it is important. In my experience, few Christians who do not tithe have ever spent time thinking about whether they could. I recommend that even if you struggle to make ends meet or are already in debt that you write out a personal or family budget that aims to pay for all your living costs and the other things that are important to your family from 90% of your income. It may not be possible for you but I suspect that it will be possible for many who just assume that it is impossible. In the next appendix, I explain how

---

[62] See Acts 20:35.

[63] Paul taught without remuneration because he wanted to go beyond his call to preach and teach, to do something more for God than what God expected of him. He explains this in 1 Corinthians 9.

to construct a budget and prioritise spending in ways that suit your circumstances.

Our giving must be fully integrated into our lives and can never be isolated from all the ways that we get and use money. After censuring some Pharisees for devouring widows' homes, Jesus went to watch how people put money into the Temple treasury. It is not always clear in translations that Jesus watched their attitudes. He may have seen some overtly show off their generosity, lingering while their coins made a loud noise clattering down into the metal containers. He may have seen others who were dutifully fulfilling their obligation to give without giving it much thought, complying with the law just because it was the right thing to do. And then a poor widow came along, easily recognised by her clothes.

I think that anyone close enough and paying any attention would have heard that she put in just two small coins. And I expect her body language suggested that it was all she had to live on. 'Truly, I tell you', Jesus told his disciples, 'this poor widow has put in more than all of them.' He did not say, more than *any* of the wealthy donors but more than *all* of them![64]

The money given by the widow in her devotion, although it was trivial in material terms, was more valuable to God than everything given by the wealthy people. This is why we must be careful that *all* the ways in which we get and use money conform to Jesus' teaching. If it does not, all our giving really does not amount to much and may not achieve much in God's service.

---

[64] See Mark 12:38-44 & Luke 20:45-21:4. Incidentally, might the widow's home and belongings have been repossessed by a Pharisee?

APPENDIX: HOW TO CONTROL MONEY

Although this book seeks to set out a framework for living in a consumer society, rather than explain the practical skills needed, I thought that an introduction to those skills might be useful to some readers. But I need to begin with a warning!

Controlling money is a life skill that we must practise if we want to do it well. We cannot learn to drive a car safely just by reading a book or listening to someone explain how to do it. *We must actually do it.* Nobody can learn to drive safely without driving a real car along real roads. And as we are certain to do some things badly and judge things poorly as we gain experience, we must be prepared to learn from our mistakes. It is the same with handling money successfully. I can explain the basic strategy but the only way to become proficient is by handling real money in real life!

Be Real

To control your money, you need to start a spending diary. This may sound like a lot of trouble but there really is no alternative and it could be life-changing. You may be surprised at just how much you spend on things that are not really important for you or your family, like sweets, coffees and magazines. And the things that catch your eye in shop windows and on internet sites that you do not use much. You may begin to see that there is a gap between the sort of person that you think you are and the sort of person you really are. You may come to realise the extent to which you are influenced by the assumptions and norms of the consumer society, which gets to us all from time to time.

Carry a piece of paper with you to write down everything you spend. Do not think that you will remember at the end of a day but write down purchases as you go. Include what you buy with debit and credit cards.

Get Organised

Every couple of days, transfer the information from your spending diary to a permanent record and sort your spending into these three categories.

- Survival costs: the things you cannot avoid paying for.
- Lifestyle choices: the things that make life more pleasant.
- Impulse spending: the things you buy on the spur of the moment but really are not important to you.

I explain more about these categories later. Once a week or once a month, whichever is more convenient for you, add into your record all your regular bills, like taxes, mortgage or rent, water, electricity and gas, travel costs, car maintenance, subscriptions and anything else. Now you can begin to draw up your first spending plan.

Check Your Income

The first step to planning your spending is to know how much money you will have. Think about where your money comes from and check that you are getting all that you are entitled to.

- Is your employer calculating your wages, overtime, tips, bonuses or commission correctly? (It is worth checking because everybody can make mistakes.)

- Is your employer paying you the full amount and not making deductions for things that you should not have to pay for?
- Are you paying the correct taxes and other mandatory contributions to your government?
- If you are unemployed or on a low income, are you entitled to any financial help from the State? Check to find out.

All your income must go into your spending plan. If you are paid weekly, plan for one week at a time. If you are paid monthly, plan monthly.

Examine Your Spending

Think about where your money goes and try to reduce what you spend. Examine each of the spending 'categories' that I mentioned earlier.

- Minimise what you spend on survival costs. You cannot avoid buying food, clothes, electricity, travel to and from work and many other things but you can reduce the cost of some. For example, eating out is more expensive than preparing meals at home. Maintaining your car properly should reduce fuel and repair costs.
- Prioritise your lifestyle choices. Few people can have it all: holidays, nights out, film and music downloads, gaming, gambling, designer clothes, cosmetics, jewellery and all the rest. Choose what is important to you and your family. Do not give into vanity by allowing what others have and do to dictate your choices.
- Limit your impulse spending. We can spend a lot on small things like coffees and magazines that we buy on a whim, without giving it much thought. Of course, occasionally, if we can afford

to, it is okay to buy a treat just because we would enjoy it. But we all need to set ourselves limits because we can spend money only once.

Make sure that you spend less than you get – it is the only way to come out ahead. Routinely adding extra spending on to overdrafts and credit cards only accumulates debt for the future. (I explain more about credit later.) Remember to put aside enough money to pay on time and in full the bills that come every three months and once a year.

Search online for free budget calculators that will help you. Or draw up a list for each category, putting what you spend in order of priority. When you prioritise your survival costs, do not try to decide whether food, for example, is more important that rent or electricity. Instead, give higher priority to the costs you have least control over. Your rent is probably fixed and you cannot alter it. So are your taxes and your travel costs to and from work. But you have some control over what you spend on food and clothes, so these come lower down your list.

Plan Your Shopping

The toughest thing about sticking with a spending plan is resisting the advertising and peer pressure that tries to convince us that we need certain things in order to be happy, liked and successful. Clothes and cosmetics are sold as if they can transform our social lives! Everything from expensive televisions to everyday food and drink can be made to seem the key to happy families! Of course, we realise it is fantasy but, even so, we can be hooked. Here is some advice.

- Never go shopping to unwind or to cheer yourself up. Shopping is **not** a leisure activity! Go shopping only when you need to.
- When you visit a supermarket, take a shopping

list. Supermarkets are designed to tempt us to buy more than we need or want but having a written shopping list helps to keep us focused on what is important.

- Check that supermarket special offers really are special. Fruit and vegetables are sometimes sold cheaper by overall weight and sometimes by unit. Large packs of things are sometimes more expensive than a number of smaller packs that add up to the same weight. And think carefully before buying 'three for the price of two', especially if you only wanted one to begin with!
- Before you buy expensive items, like furniture, kitchen appliances and televisions, be clear about what you want and how much you can afford. Take the time necessary to research the prices in different shops and internet sites. You can spend money only once and what you save on one thing can pay for something else.
- Sales staff like to 'upgrade' customers to more expensive options and get us to buy accessories. Do not allow yourself to be talked into spending money on things that are not important to you.
- Make some personal space in which to make choices. How you spend your money is up to you, not your friends, neighbours, work colleagues, advertisers or sales staff.

You will gradually get used to the discipline you impose on yourself, so that what at first is painstaking and time consuming gradually develops new habits. It is like dieting to lose weight or to address a health issue: counting the calories and learning to go without are not ends in themselves but stepping stones to a healthier lifestyle. So counting every single penny and cent should help you to evolve new ways of thinking and spending.

Think Seriously About Saving

Farmers have always put aside enough of their produce to last for the foreseeable future and we should be just as shrewd with the money we earn. Saving can help to make your life easier and more relaxed.

- You will be better prepared for the unpleasant things that happen to us all from time to time. Losing your job, having an accident or having something break down will not necessarily cause a financial crisis that adds to your problems.
- You will be ready if opportunity knocks. If you unexpectedly get the chance to fulfil a dream, you will be free to accept and will not have to worry about borrowing.
- You will be able to enjoy the special times of the year that are particularly expensive, like Christmas and birthdays, without risking a debt hangover.
- You might be able to save on some insurances if you have savings that you can use to pay for something damaged, lost or stolen.

Do not be tempted to get a savings account that charges you penalties if you withdraw money within a fixed period. Although these usually give higher rates of interest, your first savings account should allow you instant access to your money in case you underestimate a bill or have an emergency.

- Arrange to transfer a regular amount from your banking account into a separate savings account each month. Start small and try over time to build up to 15% of your income.
- Set yourself the target of saving enough money to live on for at least three months.

Adjust Your Plan

It will probably take a few months for you to develop a spending plan that works for you. But once you have it, you should be able to monitor it in about 20 minutes each week. That is the time it will take you to look at what you have spent the previous week and check that you have enough to spend in the coming week and month. And to check that your bills have been calculated accurately and that the amounts on your bank and credit statements are correct. It will also help you to reflect on your spending habits: as with driving, we can always improve!

This routine will identify any problems you have, like accidental overspending, a direct debit taking too much money from your account or identity theft. You will begin to recognise problems waiting to happen, like a routine bill that you might not be able to pay. You will then have time to adjust your other spending to deal with the problem in a controlled way. You could, if necessary, look at borrowing money as cheaply as possible, rather than having to fall back on a relatively expensive type of credit, such as overdrafts and credit cards. Or, if it is a problem that you cannot deal with yourself, you will have time to get expert help from a free advice agency.

Ration Credit

Some people say that all credit is actually debt but this is not helpful. In the past, people paid milk deliverers, grocers and other traders once a week or once a month but they were not considered to be in debt unless they could not pay on the agreed day. We need to be just as realistic today. People put groceries and other regular purchases on their credit cards and routinely pay off the total each month but do not consider themselves to be in debt. If you have the self-discipline not to use credit cards to buy what you cannot afford, they are a useful tool to help you control your money.

But please remember this! Credit is one of the easiest ways to lose control of your money. While credit cards can be useful, if you do not pay off the total balance in full each month, they are expensive credit. If you want to pay for something over two or more months, then you should think about getting a loan with a lower interest rate. But, even then, *any* unpaid credit can quickly plunge you into serious debt and make life miserable! You should therefore only borrow to buy something important.

If you think that you really have no alternative but to borrow, take some quality time to think through these questions.

- *Can I afford all the repayments?* Will you still be able to pay when you go on holiday or after Christmas?
- *Is it worth it?* As borrowing increases the cost of what we buy, do you want to pay extra? Forget the interest rate for the moment: just add up all the instalments and see if the basic price plus the interest is still a fair price to pay!
- *Will I end up paying for something I've stopped using?* For example, paying for a new television over a year may be worth it, because you will be using it all that time, but paying for a DVD over a few months is probably unwise, because you will probably watch it only once or twice!
- *Could I cope if I missed a payment?* Even if you miss one payment by just one day, default penalties and charges could be added to what you owe! Could you end up with debt you cannot repay that gets worse and worse as more penalties and charges are added?

Redundant Credit

Redundant credit is credit that you pay interest for but which is doing you no good at all. This includes continuing to pay for meals and entertainment and for things that you have stopped using. You are, in fact, paying only for memories. Even if you can make the minimum repayments comfortably, you should plan to reduce the cost of your redundant credit as quickly as possible. This will reduce your vulnerability to debt and the money you save will be like giving yourself a pay rise.

File Your Papers

When you have checked that your bills and statements are correct, file them where nobody else can see them. File your tax statements and any other letters from local and central government agencies. File them all safely. Keep them in a locked drawer. Leaving them lying around can be as foolish as leaving cash! People take them and sell them on to criminals who use the information in them to steal your identity, either to get access to your accounts or to borrow pretending to be you, so that you are expected to pay it back. That is why, when you throw away papers, you should shred them.

Occasionally, go over your bills to see if you could switch to cheaper suppliers.

Keep At It

When we have learned to drive well, we can adapt to any car in any situation. We might not like driving in a congested inner city or along winding country roads but we can adapt. When we get a new car, the controls are slightly different but we quickly get used to them. New traffic signs and road markings soon become familiar. So it is with handling money. Once you have mastered the basic skills, you can apply them to different situations.

The same skills are needed by a single person living alone, house mates and families. Our priorities may change but we can adjust our spending plan to new situations, new challenges and new financial products. But always go carefully. If you need it, get expert help. See if a local community group or advice agency offers budget coaching or organises self-help groups.

Please remember that this appendix is a basic introduction to controlling your money. I have written a book called, *Money: The Small Print*, which explains much more, including choosing banking and saving accounts, how credit works, reducing redundant credit, debt strategies, pensions, insurance, identity theft and the importance of making a will.

If you are a Christian, think about what I wrote in the appendix on giving: try to plan to live on 90% of your income, so that you can give 10%. But remember that it is just as important to look after yourself properly, care for your family and meet your financial obligations.

APPENDIX: BUSINESS IS BUSINESS

In 1776, the philosopher Adam Smith published the first modern economic theory, *The Wealth of Nations*. While he saw that people were motivated to trade not to benefit others but for personal gain, he also believed that any business that ceased to serve its community lost the right to exist. Would he be appalled at the way products are now confected only to trade on people's fears and feed their addictions?

In the 18th Century, when an investor was described as 'a man of business', because of his diverse business interests, the designation carried with it the faint odour of disreputability! A merchant, even one trading in a wide variety of goods, had about the same social rank and respect as a farmer owning his own land, because they both worked for themselves, providing goods and services to the community in order to make the money their families needed to live. But to make money for its own sake as a 'man of business', investing in anything and everything that would turn a profit, was seen as indulging the sin of avarice, the love of money, which people then still thought to be the root of all evil.

For over 100 years, there has been a widening gap between what we deem to be appropriate behaviour in everyday life and what is believed to be necessary in order to succeed in business. 'Business is business' was originally the English title of a French play written in 1903 and it very quickly came to express the assumption that society's usual standards of personal morality do not apply to business

A few years after the play was first performed in London, Dr G Campbell Morgan (who was then the Minister of Westminster Chapel, close to the theatre), said, 'I am sometimes told that, that business is business! That means that business is rascality'. That is how I am used to hearing the phrase used, to excuse pretence, duplicity and treachery. A few years ago, I was talking to the head of a professional association about a planned revision to its members' code of conduct. When I said that it should embrace legal and ethical standards of behaviour, he turned to me and said, 'What have ethics to do with this?'

Everyone in business wants to be efficient. Obviously! But the need to standardise behaviour in the cause of efficiency too often commoditises human potential and leads to exploitation. Whether it is employees or customers, once they are dealt with statistically, in the pursuit of productivity, moral and ethical restraints are weakened and breached. This is why many workers have to endure not only low wages but unsafe and unhealthy conditions; it is why modern human rights and industry codes of conduct are no defence against the profit motive!

While there are businesspeople who knowingly act illegally and unethically, there are many more who suppose, *in so much as they think about it at all*, that they are operating within industry norms, doing only what everybody else does. Their personal values are regularly tested, then shelved, because in any contest between profit and principle, profit prevails. Everybody expects it, even those who question the wisdom of it. This is why it takes so long for undesirable business practices and dishonesty to be exposed and, when subjected to public scrutiny, why those involved often fail to understand what all the fuss is about. Some readers may therefore find it thought-provoking to consider further how Jesus' financial paradigm shapes and guides business activities.

To avoid misunderstanding, I should repeat that I am not critical of business as the means for people to make money. I am not critical of the private ownership of the means of production and distribution. As I explained in Chapter 1, people have always traded for profit. But capitalism, the primacy of the profit motive, is contrary to Jesus' teaching. I invite you to reflect on three key issues found in the Sermon on the Mount: integrity (Matthew 5:33-37), relationships (Matthew 5:38-44) and society (Matthew 6:1-4). Jesus said this about integrity.

> *Again you have heard that it was said to those of old, 'You shall not swear falsely, but shall perform to the Lord what you have sworn'. But I say to you, Do not take an oath at all, either by heaven, for it is the throne of God, or by the earth, for it is his footstool, or by Jerusalem, for it is the city of the great King. And do not take an oath by your head, for you cannot make one hair white or black. Let what you say be simply 'Yes' or 'No'; anything more than this comes from evil.*

Jesus advocated plain speaking in every situation but today we are no more logical or respectable in the ways we excuse deceit than the Pharisees' system of honesty based on oaths. Historically, philosophers and theologians have limited legitimate lies to preserving the peace and maintaining adequate modesty and privacy. There are examples of justified lies in the Bible, such as the Hebrew midwives ordered by the Egyptian authorities to murder male Israelite babies but who, instead, reported that they arrived too late for the birth.[65] But in the 18th Century, the philosopher Immanuel Kant asserted that it is better to maintain a commitment to the truth rather than to lie even in a worthy cause. Since then, gradually, society has come to believe that to mislead with partial truth is not

---

[65] Exodus 1:15-21.

somehow dishonest.

Today, people blag, distract, trick, mislead, misdirect, distort, evade, bilk, fabricate, exaggerate and embellish but we do not lie; we mix euphemism, abstraction, expectation, understatement, metaphor and slang to create an illusion that cannot be sustained under scrutiny. But we do not lie. And so, whatever it is we do, we do not lie in advertising and at sales pitches, in performance reports and on helplines. In fact, it is deemed unprofessional to accuse people of lying, even when it is obvious that would have been the judgement of previous generations!

More than that, we celebrate the commercially successful and financially astute businesspeople who personify vanity, pride, greed and mendacity. We even continue when they are embroiled in scandal because success, we think, is everything! Especially if they do it with flair. The issue today is not what is legal or moral but what is achievable without penalty, doing the sorts of things many people wish they could get away with. Society only turns on them when something catches the collective imagination that people are not quite ready to forgive, like the journalists who hacked a murdered girl's mobile and provoked a judicial public inquiry into the practices and morals of the UK press in 2011.

Integrity goes beyond honesty. It includes personal wholeness, general soundness and being true to yourself and to your values. And, alongside that, it is seeking to ensure that your values are real and true and not just convenient for the time being. While it is possible to lie with integrity, it is usually the case that even white lies hurt the liars themselves. They become accustomed to fabrication that progressively collects a fog of delusion around them.

Those organisations and their employees often survive the reputational damage of exposed deceit: like so many celebrity footballers repeatedly penalised for fouls, they pay their fines and carry on as before. But trust is eroded, even if we cannot quite see it happening. Within organisations, commonly accepted standards of mendacity leave workers unable to trust their colleagues, undermining authenticity because everyone has to resort to playing a role. But employees unable to be themselves cannot be their best.

Dishonesty and inauthenticity are therefore self-defeating business norms that contaminate all our relationships. Jesus said this.

> *You have heard that it was said, 'An eye for an eye and a tooth for a tooth.' But I say to you, Do not resist the one who is evil. But if anyone slaps you on the right cheek, turn to him the other also. And if anyone would sue you and take your tunic, let him have your cloak as well. And if anyone forces you to go one mile, go with him two miles. Give to the one who begs from you, and do not refuse the one who would borrow from you.*
>
> *You have heard that it was said, 'You shall love your neighbour and hate your enemy.' But I say to you, Love your enemies and pray for those who persecute you...*

For the word 'enemy', substitute 'competitor' and 'rival'. By telling us to love these people, Jesus was including the companies we contend with for contracts and market share and the colleagues who are pursuing the same promotions and bonuses we are. Would applying his standard mean that Christians should simply 'roll over'? Obviously not.

No matter how badly people behave towards us, we have an obligation to God to act positively and constructively. When our colleagues and rivals use tactics that are unscrupulous – manipulating statistics, hiding resources, imitating products, laying claim to others' achievements, starting rumours – rather than 'give as good as we get', we should hold off posturing and act with calm and dignity. We may need to allow our temper to cool, to make time for proper analysis. We ought to act creatively and ingeniously, as well as boldly.

The original idea of competition was striving together. It was not quite as caricatured by the sentiment, *taking part is more important than winning*, because competitors always strove to be the best. But winning by any means was not only dishonest and dishonourable, it was not really winning at all! Of course, business is not sport. But the modern business obsession with winning at all costs is ultimately self-defeating. The feeding frenzy for success, the blind belief that the survival of the fittest is the way of all life and the dog-eat-dog mentality they stimulate relentlessly lowers standards of morality. It forces ever wider the gap between those who are seen as successful and the rest, so that in the end only impersonal monopolies are left.

Consider what should be the straightforward matter of bribery – what I understand the Japanese word for translates literally as 'dark mist'. Bribes are sometimes hidden in commissions and facilitation payments but around the world accepted euphuisms include references to innocent triviality, lubricants and respect. Even in countries where bribery is not the accepted social norm, it may be customary to keep potential business clients happy in order to sweeten a deal. The incentives are not necessarily cash but include expressions of friendship such as gifts luxurious hospitality and lavish entertainment.

Depending on their situation and how they view their own capabilities, people justify bribery as a necessary evil, simple pragmatism, being cleverer than most – or even as altruism![66] But, in the end, it is simply a matter of trying to induce or reward improper behaviour!

How is a Christian to handle expectations of bribery? In some business environments, corporate success is simply deemed to be more important than legal restrictions and social responsibility. Some theologians distinguish between a bribe that persuades someone to do what they should do in any event, which bribe they say is not sin, and a bribe which persuades them to do something illegal or immoral, which they think is sin! I see that distinction but all bribery is intended to make something happen that would not otherwise happen.

Leaving aside the difficult social issues of bribery to avoid unjustified harm, such as violence and false imprisonment, we focus on the impact of bribery on business. All bribery is corrupt and erodes trust. Quality of goods and service begin to matter less than the payoffs; bribery undermines the rule of law, rewards immorality, damages confidence, compromises judgement, marginalises merit, demoralises staff and stunts creativity. But what to do? I can only pose a difficult question for Christians to think on. *Can God's favour achieve more than a bribe?*

Without any better need to strive than profit, the prime motivation for businesspeople is greed! We should therefore think about the role of business in society, serving people's interests rather than exploiting their flaws. Jesus said this.

> *Beware of practicing your righteousness before other people in order to be seen by them, for then you will have no reward from your Father who is in heaven. Thus, when you give to the needy, sound*

---

[66] You may think a bribe is helping a poorly paid public official or business representative who struggles in poverty to look after his or her family properly.

no trumpet before you, as the hypocrites do in the synagogues and in the streets, that they may be praised by others. Truly, I say to you, they have received their reward. But when you give to the needy, do not let your left hand know what your right hand is doing, so that your giving may be in secret. And your Father who sees in secret will reward you.

At first glance, the above passage may seem to be about charity: acts of undeserved kindness, like gifts of money or food, offered contrary to the usual exchange of money for goods and services. This is not, however, as Jesus intended because he was talking about the rule of life, not exceptions to the rule.

I have already explored many of the parables that Jesus of Nazareth told to illustrate his teaching about money and wealth and it is clear that, in God's sight, responsibility to meet need extends far beyond the immediate commercial interests of the business, far beyond the needs of the workforce or even their families, to embrace the entire community.

While it is true that any business that fails to trade at a profit cannot serve its community, when the profit motive is supreme our very humanity is compromised. And as I explained in Chapter 3, the belief among many Christians that financial issues are outside the scope of Christian teaching is itself evidence of avarice.

In the sermon that G Campbell Morgan quoted 'business is business',[67] he went on to display remarkable foresight about the way that businesses divorced from

---

[67] 'England and the Bible', a sermon preached by G Campbell Morgan at Westminster Chapel and published the following week, on 14 April 1911, in *The Westminster Pulpit*. His reference to 'religion' was, as was usual at the time, to Christianity alone and was not meant to include other religions.

traditional Christian values would progressively dominate society.

> *When a man objects to the preacher interfering in business, I know him to be a rogue. Unless business be permeated with the principles of righteousness and integrity, unless there abide in the business life of the age, all those great conceptions which have made us free, then business will become tyranny of all tyrannies the worst. We need to remember that business is business; but that business without religion is sin, because it issues not merely in the forgetfulness of God, but in the forgetfulness of the rights of man.*

APPENDIX: A CHURCH IN NEED OF RENEWAL

Revelation, the last book in the Bible, reveals things about the world that we could not know any other way.[68] It was originally written for seven churches in Asia Minor and begins with the author, John, meeting the Lord Jesus Christ and writing down letters from him to those churches (Revelation 2-3). These letters reveal failings and iniquity in most of the churches but, in my opinion, this passage from the last of the letters is the most disturbing.

> *For you say, I am rich, I have prospered, and I need nothing, not realising that you are wretched, pitiable, poor, blind, and naked. I counsel you to buy from me gold refined by fire, so that you may be rich, and white garments so that you may clothe yourself and the shame of your nakedness may not be seen, and salve to anoint your eyes, so that you may see.*

Is it possible for a church, a fellowship of Christians, to think itself rich but in fact be impoverished? Can Christians really think themselves to be wealthy and needing nothing but actually be destitute: literally, 'wretched, miserable, poor, blind and naked'?

I doubt that a community of squatters living in poverty can ever think of themselves as wealthy. Those with mental health issues may perceive themselves as rich but

[68] The book is also known at The Apocalypse, a word associated with catastrophe but which originally meant to uncover.

that is a different problem. Some of the homeless people and squatters I have met liked their way of life and did not want permanent homes but, as content as they were, none of them believed they were materially rich!

The passage is in a letter addressed to the church in Laodicea, which is in modern Turkey. Its ruins indicate a town founded by Roman citizens, where rich people aspired to Greek culture. Paul mentioned it in his letter to the church at Colossae, asking that their letter be copied on to Laodicea and that the Colossians read the letter he sent to Laodicea. I infer from this that the letters were in some way complementary and that the churches were at about the same stage of spiritual growth. But Jesus' letter exposes how the city culture had influenced the church at Laodicea and compromised the Christians' discipleship. They had allowed their heavenly calling to be blurred by a worldly value system.

The Christians at Laodicea did not tolerate any particular heresy or evil, like some of the other churches that received letters. At Pergamum, for example, some Christians held 'the teaching of Balaam', who had used his spiritual gift for material gain. Some others were Nicolaitans, mystics who sought spiritual enlightenment through secret, enigmatic rituals. At Thyatira, they tolerated a Jezebel-type teaching that lured the Christians into sexual immorality and idolatry. Although the Christians at Laodicea were not spiritually dead, like the church at Sardis, their faith had become lukewarm. In this, they had no excuse, because they did not suffer intense persecution like the churches at Sardis and Philadelphia.

The church at Laodicea seems, however, to have been the worst of all the seven churches. The word 'wretched' in the letter should be translated with great force. Jesus called the church, '*the* wretched one'! They were in such a bad state, they were in imminent danger of divine correction and rejection!

Of all the letters that Jesus dictated, the one to Laodicea may be the most urgent message for our generation. One interpretation of the seven churches is that they represent seven phases of church history, the period that the New Testament writers often refer to as 'the last days'. The church at Laodicea, as the seventh and last church, characterises churches in the days immediately before Jesus returns, a period of time that many Christians refer to as the end times. There may be support for this idea in that Revelation describes Babylon, a global financial system, as the last stronghold to fall before the end of time.[69]

While I think there is merit in this understanding, I am sure that the seven churches are also typical of churches that have always existed in various places at various times. It follows that whether you believe that Laodicea represents the end times or not, and whether or not you think we are living in the end times, it is a sad fact that many churches today seem to be just as deluded as the one at Laodicea and need to heed the same warning.

It is amazing that there is so much hope in Jesus' letter to Laodicea! This is the full text (Revelation 3:14-22).

> *The words of the Amen, the faithful and true witness, the beginning of God's creation.*
>
> *I know your works: you are neither cold nor hot. Would that you were either cold or hot! So, because you are lukewarm, and neither hot nor cold, I will spit you out of my mouth. For you say, I am rich, I have prospered, and I need nothing, not realising that you are wretched, pitiable, poor, blind, and naked. I counsel you to buy from me gold refined by fire, so that you may be rich, and white garments*

[69] This event is so important that, after John heard about it (Revelation 14:8), an angel took him to see it in detail, described in Revelation 17-18.

so that you may clothe yourself and the shame of your nakedness may not be seen, and salve to anoint your eyes, so that you may see. Those whom I love, I reprove and discipline, so be zealous and repent. Behold, I stand at the door and knock. If anyone hears my voice and opens the door, I will come in to him and eat with him, and he with me. The one who conquers, I will grant him to sit with me on my throne, as I also conquered and sat down with my Father on his throne.

He who has an ear, let him hear what the Spirit says to the churches.

I suspect that if we were able to visit Laodicea, most of us would not see much wrong with the church. I will describe what I mean in contemporary ways. I imagine we would find it meeting in a modern building that was well-maintained with comfortable seats, air-conditioning and heating. The worship, whether 'traditional' or 'contemporary', would be well produced. The intercessions would be meaningful and the preaching relevant. We would be able to purchase not just books and sermon recordings but also ornaments, jewellery, pens, bumper stickers and a variety of other merchandise branded especially for Christians.

There would be support groups and social clubs where we could meet people we could relate to and who would make good friends. We would be encouraged to attend classes that equip us for some aspect of the church's ministry, like music, cookery, counselling, accounting and office admin. We might well find help dieting, giving up smoking, managing our money and improving our employability and career prospects.

If I am right about this, it would say as much about our superficiality as about the Laodiceans! While we must not underestimate the benefits of these things, in themselves they can be church for the consumer age: a form of

Christianity to satisfy the desires of the flesh, the desires of the eyes and the pride of life.

Looking beneath the prosperity, Jesus saw that Christianity at Laodicea was superficial. It was neither devoutly loyal nor seriously profane. Jesus could see this in their behaviour: 'I know your works: you are neither cold nor hot'. I expect the congregation would be like the people Jesus described in his Sermon on the Mount who prophesied, exorcised demons and did many mighty works using his name but who did not know him (Matthew 7:21-23). Their prosperity had made them tepid.

The Christians at Laodicea were not greedy, just complacent. They saw their material wealth as God's blessing, which is why they were content with it. We must not misunderstand their claim, quoted back to them by Jesus in the letter. 'I need nothing.' That is what they thought and in some ways it is commendable. Avarice usually breeds avarice and few rich people are content with what they have. The rich people who are content probably never had wealth as a lifestyle goal. So the Christians at Laodicea were not greedy, covetous or lovers of money. They did not necessarily want more material wealth. But, content with financial stability, they did not aspire to anything better.

They were like the seeds mentioned by Jesus in his parables of the sower that, choked by thorns, never grew to maturity: in the Laodiceans case, perhaps not choked by covetousness and the cares of this world but by the deceitfulness of riches and the pleasures of life.[70]

As I explained in Chapter 2, affluent churches should be thankful to God for comfortable buildings, minibuses, social activities and the opportunity for spiritual retreats.

---

[70] Matthew 13:1-9 & 18-23; Mark 4:1-9 & 13-20; Luke 8:5-8 & 11-15.

But if these sorts of things are all we seek from the Lord, and we are content, then something is wrong. In due course, inevitably, our belief and behaviour will be infected with mediocrity. At Laodicea, they did not realise that Jesus was altogether outside their church.

Having money is not *necessarily* evidence of God's favour. And it should not be the primary resource for any church or ministry. During the last Century, more than one preacher said that if the Holy Spirit were withdrawn from the church, most of its work would continue as if nothing had happened. I have also heard of Christians from China and Africa visiting Europe and America being amazed at how, in their opinion, the Christians achieved so much without the Holy Spirit!

Preachers may deliver sermons that sound challenging but often seek as much to satisfy as to convict. Or they may be doing nothing more than presenting their theological insights to satisfy intellectual craving, for Paul foresaw a day when Christians who could not endure sound doctrine would, nonetheless, have 'itching ears'.

The liturgy may be beautiful, sacred and profound but enacted without conviction. They may praise the God of Glory with a sincerity the people do not feel in words they do not quite believe. The worship songs may be exciting and enthusiastic but do no more than work up an atmosphere that carries the congregation through without really engaging with the God of Glory! It is neither a 'sacrifice of praise' nor a 'sacrifice of thanksgiving' because there is little or no sacrifice on the part of the worshippers, who are content to enjoy the experience.

The church may organise good works, perhaps helping the poor and homeless with food and clean clothes, but their motivation is little different to the atheists who do the same things. The Christians may demonstrate some gifts of the Holy Spirit, such as speaking in tongues and prophetic insights, but rarely do these defy a natural explanation and many prophecies linger unfulfilled and soon forgotten. They may experience miracles of healing and other remarkable answers to their prayers but only because God is unfailingly good to them and not because they are faithful to him.

The friends and work colleagues of these Christians will know they are ‘Christian’ but may not have heard them explain why. They may wear badges and jewellery that identify them as Christians and may excuse themselves from self-destructive leisure activities, such as drunkenness and sex shows. But, except that they participate in religious activities, such as attending church meetings and fellowship groups, their lifestyles may be little different. They will have the same career ambitions, desire the same lifestyle accessories, enjoy the same leisure pursuits, hold the same prejudices, maintain personal rivalries and harbour the same petty grudges.

If the Christians at Laodicea had in some sense come out of the general run of society, the ways of society were not ‘out’ of them. This is lukewarm Christianity: doctrine and lifestyle that is mundane, terrestrial, superficial, emotional and unobtrusive. It is minimalist Christianity. Whether it is ‘high church’, ‘evangelical’, ‘charismatic’ or ‘progressive’, it requires little from its congregations.

Although Jesus found nothing to commend the church at Laodicea, his letter to it is full of hope and useful guidance that remains relevant for any Christians today who can see that we, too, are lukewarm and mundane. To us, as to his people at Laodicea, Jesus says, ‘Buy from me gold refined by fire...white garments...and salve to anoint your eyes’. These are not things that can be bought with money but only by Christian discipleship. And discipleship always comes at a price!

- Gold is a symbol of devotion, persistent faith and divinity. For Laodicea and for us, it represents making the hard lifestyle choices of Christian discipleship. The place to start is time alone with God in worship, prayer and Bible reading, and time with other Christians in worship, prayer, study and fellowship. But this is not all that discipleship entails. Tough lifestyle choices must follow, to help us towards the goal of discipleship, to be more like Jesus. Take some time to go back over the difficult questions presented in this book.

- White robes symbolise truth, purity, righteousness and holiness. When three disciples saw Jesus transfigured, 'his clothes became white as light', conveying something of his divinity.[71] The martyrs and worshippers in Revelation 3 & 7 wear white. To wear white in this world, God's people should seek the Kingdom of God and God's righteousness above all other priorities. Jesus described what this means in his Sermon on the Mount. Only a faith radical enough to underwrite our dependence on God for everything we need in this world will suffice.
- Ointment is a type of healing oil that represents the Holy Spirit and the eye ointment Jesus offered allows his disciples to see clearly. It can heal the mental, emotional and spiritual wounds of materialism. It clears our view of the norms of capitalism and consumerism that we take for granted. It enables us to see Jesus' way of living in difficult times.

'Behold, I stand at the door and knock.' This is what Jesus told the church at Laodicea. Already excluded from the world when the political and religious rulers crucified him, and now excluded from his own church by the people

[71] Matthew 17:1-13.

he died to save, Jesus waits and knocks. This image inspired the famous picture by William Holman Hunt called, *The Light of the World*. It shows Christ standing at a door that has been closed for so long that weeds are beginning to obscure it. There is no handle on the outside for Christ to let himself in. But Jesus waits…and waits. This is often used in evangelism to encourage people to commit to Jesus, to let him into their lives for the first time, but Jesus' invitation was to a community of people who were already Christian.

To those who respond positively, Jesus promises intimacy with himself and responsibility in the Kingdom of God. 'If *anyone* hears my voice and opens the door', he promised, 'I will come in to *him* and eat with *him*, and *he* with me… I will grant *him* to sit with me on my throne…' The original Greek words translated as if referring only to men actually refers to male and female without distinction.

The invitation is addressed to everyone at Laodicea and could not be more general! 'If *anyone* hears my voice…' It does not matter what anyone else does or what the majority of the church decides. 'If anyone hears my voice and opens the door, I will come in to him and eat with him, and he with me.' That is intimate fellowship with Jesus!

But there is more! Fellowship with Jesus creates the potential for responsibility in the Kingdom of God. 'The one who conquers, I will grant him to sit with me on my throne, as I also conquered and sat down with my Father on his throne.' This promise is not something for eternity only, after we have died and left this world. It is available to us now. And when we can be trusted with it, people around us will not fail to see that Jesus is Lord.

Jesus was not waiting for the church leadership at Laodicea to lead; he was not even waiting for just two or three Christians to agree. If just one responded, he or she could enter into a new experience of communion and responsibility. And two or three united in this would have exponential importance. It is no different today.

> *He who has an ear, let him hear what the Spirit says to the churches.*

'One who is faithful in a very little is also faithful in much, and one who is dishonest in a very little is also dishonest in much. If then you have not been faithful in the unrighteous mammon, who will entrust to you the true riches?'

Jesus Christ of Nazareth

WHY I SELF-PUBLISH

I published my first book, *Fleeing Babylon*, in 2002. When I sent a copy of the manuscript to a friend in America, one who had written many books during his long ministry, he quickly responded that it was a good book but I needed to publish it myself in order to 'get the message out'. This advice did not appeal to me at all! I saw publishing my own work as 'vanity publishing' and it was not something that I was prepared to do.

The first publisher I approached returned the manuscript with a polite rejection slip. Another friend who had read my manuscript, and who had written many books for the same publisher, sent it back with a personal request for the director responsible for Christian books to reconsider. The note that came back was both encouraging and daunting: it said that my book was well written but that Christians do not read books about money and so even a low volume print run would not make a profit.

I sent the manuscript to another publisher. It came straight back, almost by return post, obviously unread and with a note explaining that the publisher already had a self-help book about money to publish 'next year'. *Next year!*

At about this time, I listened to a tape from a Christian conference where the speakers participated in a panel discussion. One of the questions put to them was which books besides the Bible had most influenced them. Most of the books they identified had been self-published. As that sunk in, I decided to self-publish *Fleeing Babylon*.

If I was going to be a publisher, I wanted to do it properly and so I applied for International Standard Book Numbers (ISBNs). I had to decide whether to create a publishing name or use my own name and opted for the latter. If there was a stigma to self-publishing, and if that was what I was supposed to do, then it was a stigma I would embrace gladly: most of my books say, 'Published by the author'. Everything I have published since then has been under my own name but the stigma – if ever there was one – has now entirely evaporated. Amazon and other digital publishing platforms have made it not only easy but also normal to self-publish.

Since publishing *Fleeing Babylon*, I have realised that it is the only way I want to do it. It gives me complete control over distribution, so that I can give away as many copies as I like. This was very useful when I taught personal finance in schools and I often found a company willing to sponsor the printing. In this way, the book that is now available as, *Money: The Small Print*, went through many editions. I did not give out copies indiscriminately to everyone in my audiences but I offered them to all and gave to anyone who asked for one. I believe that in this way I gave to hundreds of teenagers (and to many older people, also) something that could help them manage their futures and which, in a postscript, contained a short testimony to Jesus of Nazareth.

But there is a downside to self-publishing. The one major problem I experience is a lack professional editing and proofreading skills and to pay for these would add significantly to the publication costs. But with help from my friends, the job gets done. Sort of. (If you see a mistake in this book, please get in touch because I may have an opportunity to correct it.)

When in 2015 I had nearly finished writing my book, *Living with God and Money*, I thought again about seeking a professional publisher. I made a few enquiries but decided against it. Through the internet, I have a potential audience as wide as any publisher. Having said that, I of course recognise that a well-known publisher gives a book credibility and a profile that brings it to the attention of established national and global readerships. But I believe that if God approves of what I write, copies will find their way to people who will appreciate them. And if God does not approve, then I need to watch my step! This is why I do not do very much to proactively promote my own books: while I try to make them known to people who may be interested, I am wary of trying too hard.

I must explain that I see no problem with Christians publishing books ‘professionally’ and for profit. I would not want anyone to infer otherwise from anything that I have written. I have no criticism of that at all (except, I suppose, the very high prices sometimes charged that can be a barrier to Christians struggling on low incomes) but it is not something that I want to do. Whether I am good enough to be published ‘professionally’ remains untested but I hope there is no vanity involved in what I do. And I pray that, as my friend said in 2002 about my first book, that this latest one is an effective way to ‘get the message out’.

ABOUT THE AUTHOR

Philip Evans was born at the dawn of the consumer society: the same week as rationing was finally abolished in the UK after the Second World War and a few days before restrictions were lifted on using credit for luxury goods, which at that time included things that we now think of as essential, such as televisions, fridges and vacuum cleaners. It was the month that the UK Government announced that it wanted housewives, the people who did most shopping, to be as choosy as they liked and producers to produce what the public wanted. (In case you are wondering, all that was July 1954.) Philip became a Christian in 1968.

After a career in the UK civil service, where he first became involved in credit and debt issues, Philip worked as a consultant both for organisations responsible for collecting unpaid debt and for advice agencies working to help people in debt. He began teaching personal finance skills in 2002, mainly in schools, and from the start wanted to ensure that what he taught was consistent with what he believed as a Christian. That began a fascinating Bible study that continues today.

Philip's other books include, *Fleeing Babylon*; *Living with God & Money*; *Money: The Final Conflict*; *Sustainability & Transcendence in Business*; *Money: The Small Print*. Most of these are available from Amazon. Or check Philip's Facebook page, 'Living with God and Money'.

Printed in Poland
by Amazon Fulfillment
Poland Sp. z o.o., Wrocław

54263172R00094